W9-CEW-571

**Glorious Praise for
Robert Lanham's Books**

The Hipster Handbook

"What *The Preppy Handbook* did for whale belts and synonyms for vomiting, *The Hipster Handbook* accomplishes for this generation's stylistic and linguistic signs and signifiers . . . thoroughly entertaining."
—*The New York Times*

"Your official guide to the language, culture, and style of hipsters young and old." —*Los Angeles Times*

"Almost embarrassingly funny." —*Library Journal*

"*The Official Preppy Handbook* for people who wear Atari T-shirts."
—*Esquire*

"So comprehensive and so well-done that only a poseur could criticize it without tongue in cheek." —*Slate*

"Wonderful and frighteningly accurate." —*Gawker*

continued . . .

*Food Court Druids, Cherohonkees
and Other Creatures Unique to the Republic*

"Robert Lanham is the Margaret Mead of the North American Weirdo."

> —Neal Pollack, author of *Never Mind the Pollacks* and
> *The Neal Pollack Anthology of American Literature*

"Since Election 2004, those of us who live in major coastal metropolitan centers have been scolded about how little we understand the rest of the country. Lucky for us, Brooklyn-based trendspotter Robert Lanham . . . is on the case. . . . Forget Security Moms, NASCAR Dads, Metrosexuals. Lanham offers a panoply of new, more finely tuned idiotypes."   —*Boston Globe*

"This book is a riot."   —*The Cleveland Plain Dealer*

"[Lanham] looks beyond politics, mining the vast area between NPR and NASCAR to sweepingly and hilariously generalize about many groups of everyday people."   —*The Washington Post*

"Lanham's observational humor puts Jerry Seinfeld to shame."
          —*Times Leader*, Wilkes-Barre, PA

"Hilariously accurate descriptions of coworkers, family members, friends, and other acquaintances that almost every American has encountered."   —*Publishers Weekly*

"Will cause outright, prolonged laughter."   —*Orlando Sentinel*

The Sinner's Guide to the

EVANGELICAL RIGHT

Robert Lanham

 NEW AMERICAN LIBRARY

New American Library
Published by New American Library, a division of
Penguin Group (USA) Inc., 375 Hudson Street,
New York, New York 10014, USA
Penguin Group (Canada), 90 Eglinton Avenue East, Suite 700, Toronto,
Ontario M4P 2Y3, Canada (a division of Pearson Penguin Canada Inc.)
Penguin Books Ltd., 80 Strand, London WC2R 0RL, England
Penguin Ireland, 25 St. Stephen's Green, Dublin 2,
Ireland (a division of Penguin Books Ltd.)
Penguin Group (Australia), 250 Camberwell Road, Camberwell, Victoria 3124,
Australia (a division of Pearson Australia Group Pty. Ltd.)
Penguin Books India Pvt. Ltd., 11 Community Centre, Panchsheel Park,
New Delhi - 110 017, India
Penguin Group (NZ), cnr Airborne and Rosedale Roads, Albany,
Auckland 1310, New Zealand (a division of Pearson New Zealand Ltd.)
Penguin Books (South Africa) (Pty.) Ltd., 24 Sturdee Avenue,
Rosebank, Johannesburg 2196, South Africa

Penguin Books Ltd., Registered Offices: 80 Strand, London WC2R 0RL, England

First published by New American Library, a division of Penguin Group (USA) Inc.

First Printing, September 2006
10   9   8   7   6   5   4   3   2   1

Copyright © Robert Lanham, 2006
All rights reserved

Grateful acknowledgment is made for permission to reprint the following:

Art on page 199 reprinted by permission. *Revolve: The Complete New Testament,* 2003. Thomas
Nelson, Inc., Nashville, Tennessee. All rights reserved

Art on page 132 courtesy of MarMont Group and K&K Mime.

 REGISTERED TRADEMARK—MARCA REGISTRADA

LIBRARY OF CONGRESS CATALOGING-IN-PUBLICATION DATA:

Lanham, Robert.
    The sinner's guide to the evangelical right/Robert Lanham.
        p. cm.
    ISBN 0-451-21945-7 (trade pbk.)
    1. Evangelicalism—United States—Humor.   2. United States—Religious life and
customs—Humor.   3. Conservatism—Religious aspects—Christianity—Humor.   I. Title.
BR1642.U5L36   2006
277.3'0B30207—dc22   2006009913

Set in Fairfield and Helvetica Neue
Designed by Victoria Hartman

Printed in the United States of America

To Adrianne

"Beware of false prophets, which come to you in sheep's clothing, but inwardly they are ravening wolves."

Matthew 7:15

"There is no sin except stupidity."   *Oscar Wilde*

"I think George Bush is going to win in a walk. I really believe I'm hearing from the Lord it's going to be like a blowout election in 2004. The Lord has just blessed him. . . . It doesn't make any difference what he does, good or bad."

Pat Robertson, AP/Fox News, January 2, 2004

"God is not dead."

President George W. Bush, addressing the nation in 2006

Warning:
This book is protected by Bibleman, the evangelical Superman.

Forty-seven percent of adults in the United States—nearly half the population—claim to be born-again or evangelical. (ABCNEWS/Beliefnet poll)

Definition

Evan·gel·i·cals: *noun; pronunciation: "E-"van-'je-li-kals*
Christians who claim to have a personal relationship with Jesus Christ, think the Bible is infallible, and feel God wants them to spread His word to others. Most evangelicals are cultural conservatives who believe the Bush tax cuts were prophesied in the Bible. They enjoy the type of music one hears on *Star Search* reruns.

The term "evangelical" is often used loosely as a blanket term that includes the subsets Fundamentalists, morally strict reactionaries who prefer the Bible to things like facts, and **Pentecostals** and **Charismatics,** holy-rollin' Christians who speak in tongues and believe handling snakes is a good way to work up an appetite before visiting the Shoney's brunch buffet.

Converting the unsaved is the ultimate goal of evangelicals, since they believe doing so will hasten the Second Coming of Christ.

Senator Score Card

Before the 2006 mid-term election, forty-two senators received perfect scores from the Christian Coalition in their most recent tally, meaning they voted the way the evangelical right wanted them to 100 percent of the time:

Jeff Sessions (R-AL)
Jon Kyl (R-AZ)
Saxby Chambliss (R-GA)
Larry Craig (R-ID)
Richard Lugar (R-IN)
Pat Roberts (R-KS)
Mitch McConnell (R-KY)
Kit Bond (R-MO)
Thad Cochran (R-MS)
Conrad Burns (R-MT)
Chuck Hagel (R-NE)
John Sununu (R-NH)
John Ensign (R-NV)
George Voinovich (R-OH)
Rick Santorum (R-PA)
Lamar Alexander (R-TN)
John Cornyn (R-TX)
Robert Bennett (R-UT)
George Allen (R-VA)
Craig Thomas (R-WY)

Richard Shelby (R-AL)
Wayne Allard (R-CO)
Chuck Grassley (R-IA)
Mike Crapo (R-ID)
Sam Brownback (R-KS)
Jim Bunning (R-KY)
Norm Coleman (R-MN)
James Talent (R-MO)
Trent Lott (R-MS)
Elizabeth Dole (R-NC)
Judd Gregg (R-NH)
Pete Domenici (R-NM)
Mike DeWine (R-OH)
James Inhofe (R-OK)
Lindsey Graham (R-SC)
Bill Frist (R-TN)
Kay Bailey Hutchison (R-TX)
Orrin Hatch (R-UT)
Mike Enzi (R-WY)
former Senators Nickles, Miller, and Fitzgerald

Contents

Introduction—A Praylude
Stephen Baldwin is stalking sinners and half the Senate
is born-again. It's okay to have Evangophobia.   xix

Our Cast
Meet your tour guides for this book: a diverse group
of evangelicals and Ronnie James Dio.   xxv

Fire and Brimstone Scale   xxxiii

I: **James Dobson and an Evangelical 101 for the
Wayward Sinner**
   Meet James Dobson, the "Evangelical Pope."   1
   Brush up on your knowledge of evangelical culture:
      the denominations, church etiquette, speaking in
      tongues, text message Bibles, and ministers with goatees.   7

2: **Joel Osteen and Our Prosperity-Lovin' Megachurch
Nation**
   Meet Joel Osteen, the evangelical P. Diddy.   29
   Take a peek inside our nation's megachurches, try a burger
      in their food courts, and discover how to become a
      millionaire by following Creflo Dollar.   37

3: Rick Warren and the Seeker-Sensitive Pastorpreneurs

Meet Rick Warren, the evangelical Jimmy Buffet.   53

Discover how megachurch pastors try to trick sinners
    into believing they're cool with free gas, U2 tickets,
    and Hawaiian shirts.   59

4: The American Evangelicals: Christian by Birth, Republican by the Grace of God

Discover why God hates shrimp as much as he hates
    gays and find out how the word "*evangelical*" became
    synonymous with Republican.   73

Meet our nation's scariest evangelical leaders.   84

Interlude: Evangelical Hairdos   110

5: The Duke of Haggard and the Evangelical Vatican

Meet Ted Haggard, the tongues-speaking White
    House insider who talks to George Bush every Monday.   115

Take a "prayerwalk" through Colorado Springs, the
    so-called Evangelical Vatican.   123

6: Tim LaHate and the Impending Apocalypse

Meet Tim LaHaye, the evangelical Stephen King.   139

Find out if the Rapture is about to happen and see
    why the *Left Behind* authors think Saddam Hussein
    is the predecessor to the Antichrist.   146

7: Paul Weyrich and the Vast Right-Wing Conspiracy

Meet Paul Weyrich, the evangelical Dr. Strangelove.   159

Find out who is responsible for making Intelligent Design
    a hot-button issue and meet the key organizations that
    make up the evangelical right. Decide for yourself . . . is
    there a vast right-wing conspiracy?   167

8: Rob Bell and the Emerging Youth

Meet Rob Bell, the evangelical Steve Jobs.   183

Introduce yourself to a few evangelicals that even a
sinner can admire. Take a peek inside the "Christian
Cocoon": Bibleman, Christian Rock, and fashion
magazine Bibles.   189

Postscript: Emerging Backlash, the Other Emerging Church

Meet Mark Driscoll and discover why God hates him.   204

The Evangelical Quiz

Test your knowledge   211

Christianese

An evangelical glossary   217

Our Statement of Beliefs   227

Acknowledgments   229

Welcome to *The Sinner's Guide to the Evangelical Right*

Praylude

- *63 percent of Americans think the Bible is literally true.*
- *Lakewood Church meets in the former home of the Houston Rockets to accommodate their thirty thousand regular attendees.*
- *Focus on the Family receives so much mail they have their own zip code.*
- *79 percent of the 26.5 million evangelical voters supported Bush in the 2004 election.*

Does reading these facts make your palms sweat? Do you often wonder when Christians became pro-business Wal-Mart shoppers? Does the term "family values" conjure up nightmarish images of Pat Robertson smacking the remote control out of your hand as he sheds dandruff flakes onto the upholstery of your sofa? Are you a sinner, but worry that the "righteous" have thrown the first stone?

If you answered yes to any of these questions, you may be suffering from a disease known as *Evangophopia*. The fear of evangelicals. But don't worry; it's more common than you think. Even some moderate *evangelicals* are developing symptoms. After all, the triumph of mall-sized megachurches with Taco Bells and rock-climbing walls inside them could test the faith of a dozen holy apostles.

If you think you may have evangophobia, the good news is that you're not alone. It's a downright pandemic. An estimated 98.6 percent of all non-evangelical Americans have symptoms.

Webster's Dictionary defines a phobia as an *illogical* fear. An irrational anxiety. Let's be clear; there's nothing irrational about being afraid of an army of evangelicals dressed in flag sweaters. Especially when they seem to be taking over America. We wouldn't be surprised if the Senate began filibustering in tongues. And if you don't get anxious when a four-ton SUV passes you on the interstate with a bumper sticker that says *WARNING: In case of rapture this vehicle will be unmanned*, there's probably something wrong with you. The actor Stephen Baldwin, for God's sake, is the host of a traveling skateboarding ministry. He's been hanging out in parking lots of adult entertainment shops photographing patrons as part of an antiporn campaign.

Given these facts, we sinners are in *full agreement* with evangelicals on one major point: the Apocalypse is drawing near. Evangophobia is normal. It's a healthy fear. And we're here to help.

Megachurch Nation

The evangelical right isn't the new counterculture. It's the new mainstream culture.

For decades, evangelical Christians have been organizing. They have their own newspapers. Their own radio stations. Their own music. Their own slang. Their own paintball teams. There's an evangelical church in Texas that has its own McDonald's drive-through. And in 2005, evangelicals even created their own holiday: Ten Commandments Day.

Worst of all, many evangelicals aren't content watching *The 700 Club* and attending laser-light projections of the crucifixion at the local megachurch. They want to transform the culture you consume to fit their standards. In fact, if they're true "evangelizers" they want to transform *you* to fit their standards. And compounded by the fact that evangelicals often share similar goals with conservative Jews, Catholics,[1]

---

[1] Catholics aren't typically classified as evangelicals. Many fundamentalist Christians even have doubts about whether Catholics are saved and think following the Pope is blasphemous. Still, both evangelicals and Catholics can definitely agree on one vital point: that guy who wrote *The Da Vinci Code* is definitely going to hell.

and Bill O'Reilly, we may soon witness a ratings' sweeps plotline where Will marries Grace after attending a gay deprogramming class.

Since Bush's reelection in 2004, people have been scratching their heads trying to understand this parallel social group known as the evangelical right. Let's face facts. Most non-evangelicals don't know the difference between Ted Haggard and Merle Haggard, Pat Robertson and Pat Buchanan, or James Dobson and the cloven-hoofed demonlord of the Apocalypse.

Sinners need a guide to demystify this powerful group before this plague of evangophobia gets out of control. After all, confronting one's fears brings healing.

The Idiosyncrology of Evangelicals

Our nonprofit foundation, the American Idiosyncrology Institute, is in the business of decoding the mysteries of idiosyncratic people. This book is the culmination of our research on this ubiquitous group known as the evangelical right.

During the course of our study we attended dozens of churches across the country to observe the different styles of worship. Traditional churches are a dying breed, we discovered; almost all of the churches we visited resorted to gimmicks and sensationalism. New Life Church in Colorado, for instance, had free wi-fi Internet, fog machines, and a terrorism conference taught by the local police. Creflo Dollar's church in New York featured a thirty-minute "sermon" by a woman speaking in tongues. And West End Assembly of God in Virginia had an Easter musical with live camels.

Immersing ourselves in evangelical culture, we became temporary citizens of Colorado Springs, a town that has become known as the Evangelical Vatican. It's the home of the so-called protestant pope, James Dobson, and hundreds of "parachurch" groups—Christian organizations like Campus Crusades, Young Life, and the Christian Cowboys—that are evangelical but not church-based. It's also the home of SUVs with Jesus mudflaps and patriotic eagle statuettes.

Evangelicals have received a lot of scrutiny lately, so access was often tricky. For all their talk of inclusiveness, most are actually wary of intruders and are experts at spotting them. We found that unless you sign your e-mails "God bless" and say *"Hallelujah"* when hearing an anecdote about converting a Hasidic salesclerk at Circuit City, they'll likely identify you as an outsider.

We also found that many evangelicals are media savvy, so the persona they present to the secular Target[2] shoppers doesn't always match their behavior when among other believers. For instance, the Colorado megachurch pastor Ted Haggard (who talks politics with George Bush every Monday morning) told members of his congregation to not "be weird" when media is around. Ironically, the trampolines just outside of their sanctuary and the Starbucks café in their lobby didn't register with Haggard as being weird.

Not surprisingly, many of our undercover field researchers suffered from serious cases of performance anxiety when it came to raising their hands in the air during the worship services. Others were subjected to the trauma of being in the presence of people speaking in tongues for hours on end. And needless to say, achieving that shiny, clean-living, evangelical glow, like the members of the Christian band Jars of Clay, required incredible moral discipline for everyone involved in the study.

Most notably, we observed that, despite the clichés, not all evangelicals are alike. For every Pat Robertson and Jerry Falwell there's a Jim Wallis (p. 190) and a Brian McLaren (p. 190) doing their best to unite people, not divide them. Wallis and McLaren are living testimonies that *evangelical* isn't a synonym for *homophobic NRA-supporting Republican with a venison freezer*. You may not have heard of these kinder, gentler leaders. Teaching inclusiveness doesn't grab headlines like blaming 9/11 on the ACLU, spearheading *Christmas Friend or Foe* campaigns, or claiming, as Ted Haggard does, that pro-business capitalism is what Jesus intended.

True diversity among evangelicals *does* exist, and we'll introduce you to some of Evangelicalism's more progressive leaders, not to mention our own cast of real-life evangelicals who will be your guides

---

[2] Target has given money to Planned Parenthood. Plus, Target doesn't carry firearms or cutting-edge literature like *God, Pepsi, and Groovin' on the High Side: Tales from the NASCAR Circuit* like its more evangelical-friendly sister store, Wal-Mart.

throughout this book. Our evangelical guides, Amanda, Sam, Mike, J.J., Johane, and Dio, will provide commentary from an insider's perspective.

Despite the ministries of people like Wallis and McLaren, it's the extremists from the evangelical right who presently have the clout. They've blocked the sanctuary doors. They've hoarded the communion grape juice. They've stolen the words "family," "freedom," "patriot," and "values" and claimed them as their own. They've committed the biggest sin of all. They've kidnapped Jesus.

Promiscuity may be a sin, but they're screwing us all. They're the focus of this book.

This is *The Sinner's Guide to the Evangelical Right*.

The Tour Guides: Our Cast of Real-Life Evangelicals and Ronnie James Dio

In conducting our research, we selected six evangelical tour guides to provide insight from an insider's perspective throughout this book. Sam and Johane requested we not include their pictures. Their quotes are very much real and verbatim, but their illustrations do not represent their actual likenesses. Amanda's name has been changed. She is a lesbian who lives in a state with Right-to-Work laws, meaning she can be fired without explanation by her employer.

Sam

"Some people are predestined to not receive God's grace. . . . I'm one of God's chosen people."

Race: Caucasian
Job: Camera Salesman
Personal: Married/One kid

Born: 1967
Location: Austin, Texas
Politics: Bush supporter and Pro-Life

Religious Affiliation: Baptist
Born Again: Got serious about Jesus in his thirties

Speaks in Tongues: No, says that's "weird"
Alcohol: Likes to drink

The Rapture: Believes it will happen in his lifetime

In his twenties, Sam was a "heavy drinker" and "womanizer" before getting born again. He compares his ordeals to the troubled life of Job in the Old Testament; he had open-heart surgery when he was fifteen, his house burned down when he was twenty, he killed someone in a car accident when he was twenty-two, his father died when he was twenty-five, and he was once arrested for possessing what he calls "a party drug." Now, Sam's a churchgoing evangelical who believes he is one of "God's elected people," an individual preordained to join God in Heaven. Nevertheless, he sometimes worries his preacher might drive by and see him drinking while he's mowing the lawn. There's no way to know yet, he claims, whether his child was selected by God to go to Heaven. No liberal elitist, Sam doesn't like sushi.

Amanda

"Most people in my church wouldn't accept me if they knew I was a lesbian."

Race: Caucasian   **Born:** 1967
Job: Human Resource Director   **Location:** Williamsburg, Virginia
Personal: Serious Relationship/ No kids   **Politics:** Bush supporter and Pro-Life
Religious Affiliation: Nondenominational   **Born Again:** As a teen
Speaks in Tongues: Yes   **Alcohol:** Likes to drink
The Rapture: Doesn't believe in the Rapture

Amanda is an evangelical lesbian who lives in the heart of the Bible Belt. "Being gay isn't a sin," she says. She thinks evangelicals should focus more on helping the poor and needy. Amanda is against gay marriage but supports civil unions, because she doesn't want to "force a new definition of marriage on people who don't want it." She has "advanced gaydar" and has dated other lesbians she's met at church. She's currently in a serious relationship with a woman who used to teach a gay deprogramming class. Amanda recently came out to her fundamentalist parents, who have since stopped talking to her. Amanda likes vegetarian sushi.

Mike

"We went to the adult expo in Las Vegas . . . I kept thinking, if they find out we're Christians, they're gonna kill us."

Race: Caucasian

Job: Part-time Pastor/ Design Company Founder

Personal: Married/Two kids

Religious Affiliation: Nondenominational

Speaks in Tongues: No, not his cup of tea

Born: 1971

Location: Corona, California

Politics: Bush supporter and Pro-Life

Born Again: As a teen

Alcohol: Likes to drink

The Rapture: Believes it could occur anytime, but worrying about when it will happen is a waste of time

Mike is the founder of XXXChurch, "The number one Christian porn site." But it's nothing like it sounds. XXXChurch is an *antiporn* ministry. He experienced a supernatural "Benny Hinn moment" (p. 100) in the shower when God told him to start an antiporn crusade. "Why won't the church talk about this issue?" Mike asks, citing a statistic that 37 percent of all pastors admit to struggling with porn. In 2005, XXXChurch sponsored National Porn Sunday by sending pastors information on how to talk to their congregations about porn, including a documentary called *Missionary Positions*. He thinks people should avoid masturbating, since it involves lustful thoughts. His Web site, xxxchurch.com, offers free "accountability software" for porn addicts. Once installed, the software notifies friends with an e-mail alert whenever a user visits a porn site. Mike doesn't like sushi. His "food must be cooked."

Johane

"I'm not gonna lie, it's been tough [remaining a virgin], but that's what the Bible says to do."

Race: Haitian American

Born: 1987

Job: Spanish Major, Kennesaw State University

Location: Kennesaw, Georgia

Personal: Single/No kids

Politics: Too young to vote in 2004, Pro-Life

Religious Affiliation: Nondenominational

Born Again: When she was fifteen

Speaks in Tongues: No

Alcohol: Thinks getting drunk is wrong

The Rapture: It's not likely to happen anytime soon

Johane idolizes Oprah and Jesus, but says her mom is her true role model. When Johane's family moved from New Jersey to Georgia in 2000, they hit hard economic times. Her dad had no job and developed prostate cancer. (He's since recovered.) Her mom—who's "on fire for Jesus"—relied on her faith to find work and support the family. Johane suffered from culture shock after moving to a town with "Jesus billboards everywhere." One day, nearly everyone at her high school wore matching church youth group T-shirts. "You'd *never* see that in New Jersey," she joked. When she was younger, Johane attended a Pentecostal church where women had to wear head coverings. Still, she never took being an evangelical seriously until being inspired by her mom's faith in their hard economic times. She's currently experiencing a new culture shock at college, being surrounded by "partiers" who don't understand her commitment to God, not to mention her abstinence. Johane hates sushi.

Joseph
(a.k.a. J. J. Luz)

"When people think of evangelicals they think of Robertson and Dobson. . . . People ignore the ethnic leaders."

Race: Hispanic
Job: Trains pastors to plant and grow churches
Personal: Single/No kids

Religious Affiliation: Charismatic
Speaks in Tongues: Yes
The Rapture: It will happen any moment

Born: 1976
Location: Colorado Springs, Colorado
Politics: Bush supporter and Pro-Life
Born Again: As a teen
Alcohol: A beer is okay, getting drunk is wrong

J.J. is a "young MC with a prophetic edge." Though he attends the solidly middle-class and largely white New Life megachurch in Colorado Springs, he brings some urban flavor with his own Christian rap ministry, Illumination Productions International. His stage moniker is J.J. Luz, which means "light." Raised Catholic, J.J. began attending a Protestant church as a teen with a girlfriend. He's the son of a deadbeat dad, a heroin addict who did time in San Quentin. "He'd cut you if he needed to," J.J. says. They eventually reconciled, but in 2004 his father became ill and died of liver disease. J.J. worries he wasn't saved. While speaking with us, J.J. confessed to having been interviewed months prior by a political magazine doing a story on evangelicals. We thought it a unique coincidence, given we chose him at random from a congregation of twelve thousand. A firm believer in supernatural encounters, J.J. thinks it could be the work of God. J.J. enjoys salmon sushi.

Ronnie James Dio[3]

"When Armageddon comes, the streets shall run red with blood, a hail of bones shall fall from the sky, and there shall be nothing but *Too Close for Comfort* reruns on TV."

Race: Caucasian
Job: Devil Rocker
Personal: Bachelor, enjoys Carnival Cruises on the River Styx
Religious Affiliation: Church of cloven-hoofed goat man

Speaks in Tongues: No, but thinks forked tongues are a turn-on

Born: 1949
Location: The fiery abyss
Politics: Those of the Antichrist

Born Again: "To be born again, one must die . . . are you threatening me?"
Alcohol: Prefers painkillers

The Rapture: "I have not had a single on the radio in two decades: you bet your ass we're in the end-times!!!"

Dio is credited with popularizing the satanic horns hand gesture. He was in the bands Elf, Rainbow, Black Sabbath, and his namesake, Dio. He was born of a jackal. He sings of rainbows, and darkness, and harlequins, and is often mistaken for an elfin wizard. He's an evangelical too. For the dark one, that is. He loves sushi but prefers his meals to be alive.

---

[3] *We didn't actually interview Ronnie James Dio. We discovered his quotes by playing his album* Killing the Dragon *backwards. It's jam-packed with esoteric evangelical commentary.*

Fire and Brimstone Scale

1. Liberal, even likes the gays
2. Progressive, probably prefers Clinton and Carter to Dubya and Reagan
3. Moderate, is fond of the words "decent," "sensible," and "forgive"
4. Traditional, will tolerate them gays if they wear gloves when preparing food
5. Conservative, is fond of the words "sodomite," "Rapture," and "repent"
6. Ultraconservative, thinks Bush should have played Jesus in *The Passion of the Christ*
7. Reactionary, thinks the Antichrist shall soon take over the world unless we immediately burn all copies of the blasphemous *The Da Vinci Code*
8. Sociopath, thinks Jesus will return any day with a flamethrower

The Sinner's Guide to the
EVANGELICAL
RIGHT

James Dobson, the Evangelical Pope

James Dobson and an Evangelical 101 for the Wayward Sinner

Dr. James Dobson: The Evangelical Pope

Fire and Brimstone Score: 8

Nutshell: Founder of Focus on the Family, the most powerful evangelical ministry in the country

Denomination: Son of a Nazarene minister, Bible literalists with a strict moral code

Born: 1936

Defining Quote: "Communities do not let prostitutes, pedophiles, voyeurs, adulterers, and those who sexually prefer animals to publicly celebrate their lifestyles, so why should homosexuals get such privileges?"

Quick Facts about James Dobson
- He's a psychologist, not a minister, with zero theological training.
- He's apparently on speed dial at the White House, since he's regularly consulted by the staff there.
- He's married to Shirley Dobson, the chair-Christian of the National Day of Prayer Task Force.
- He's a founding board member of the Christian political lobby, Family Research Council.
- He routinely advised Bush's campaign advisor, Karl Rove, during the 2004 election.
- He's had a regular bowel movement right after supper for the past eight and a half years.

The Evangelical Pope

Forget Pat Robertson. Forget Billy Graham. Forget that other dude who buys his suits at the Burlington Coat Factory and says "Jay-sus." Dr. James Dobson hates the queers more vehemently than anyone in America. The chairman and founder of the Colorado Springs–based ministry known as Focus on the Family, he's also the world's most powerful evangelical leader, earning him the unofficial title the Evangelical Pope. Reportedly, Dr. Dobson even smells "Christiany." Combining folksy family psychology—Dobson has a Ph.D. in child development—with a very literal interpretation of the Bible, Dobson's nondenominational evangelical videos, newsletters, books, and radio show now reach more than 200 million people daily. That's an audience ten times larger than the population of New York State. Tellingly, Dobson was even privy to inside information on Supreme Court nominees, provided by the White House, weeks before most of the members of Congress got the information. And yes, he's the guy who thinks SpongeBob SquarePants is gay.

Focus on Your Own Family, Please

Focus on the Family began modestly in 1977 when Dobson published his first child-rearing tome, *Dare to Discipline*, and secured a weekly radio show in California. Now, his tax-exempt empire has published dozens of bestselling Christian books and Dobson's radio shows can be heard on over two hundred stations in the United States alone. His newsletter, which often discusses current political events alongside commonsense, pseudo-spiritual psychology, is readily available in the lobby of nearly every evangelical church in the country. With the exception of the buffet at Ryan's Steakhouse, nothing is more popular with evangelicals than the ministry of Dr. Dobson.

Quick Facts about Dobson's Focus on the Family

- Has an annual budget of $146 million and receives so much mail it has its own zip code.
- Distributed 8 million voting guides during the 2004 election.
- Organized boycotts against AT&T (supports gay rights), Procter & Gamble (supports gay rights), Disney (supports gay rights), and Abercrombie & Fitch (ran sexy ads, but probably supports gay rights too).

- Has fourteen hundred employees and answers thousands of calls daily at its Christian counseling hotline.
- Dobson secretly wants to change the company's name to Focus on the Fags.

I would like to say James Dobson is naught but a Hypocrite Wyrm suckled on Beelzebub's teat, a Serpentine shill for a false God, but I'd hate to stop receiving those lovely Hickory Farms Gift Baskets every Winter Solstice.

"Pain Is a marvelous purifier"

Ironically, given his gentle demeanor and the softness of his hands (Dobson moisturizes them lovingly every morning with a greaseless hand lotion before doing his Rapture exercises), Dobson began his career by publishing a book about spanking. *Dare to Discipline* is his response to what he believes to be a culture of permissive parenting. In it, he promotes the disciplinary effectiveness of spanking, even for "sick and deformed" children, whom, he says, should be treated no differently than normal children. After all, his own mother hit him with "a multitude of straps and buckles," and look how normal James turned out! Dobson says he believes spanking is biblical. Everyone knows that Mary spanked Jesus with a bamboo reed whenever he turned his brussels sprouts into Reese's Pieces.

Highlights from Dobson's *Dare to Discipline* and *The Strong-Willed Child*

"[P]ain is a marvelous purifier. . . . There is a muscle, lying snugly against the base of the neck. . . . When firmly squeezed, it sends little messengers to the brain saying, 'This hurts; avoid recurrence at all costs.'"

"I suggest [spanking with] a switch (a small, flexible twig from a tree) or a paddle . . . if it doesn't hurt it doesn't motivate."

Rejected Titles for *Dare to Discipline*

- A Dummy's Guide to Sticks, Spatulas, Belts, Switches, and Ping-Pong Paddles
- Spare the Rod, Spoil the Demon-Possessed Hellion
- Just Wait 'til Your Father Gets Home (He's Hungry, Overworked, and Ready to Kick Some Ass)
- Spanking the Fairy Out of Him
- Paddle off the Pounds: The Spanker's Diet
- Everybody Hurts, Sometimes
- Speak Softly and Carry a Viny Switch
- Spank Liberally, Vote Conservatively
- If You Can't Beat 'Em, Give 'Em a Good Shaking
- Take That, You Godless Little Shit. Do You Want Another? DO YA?!
- The Jesus Paddle

QUICK QUIZ: What does Dobson call children who may be on the path to becoming gay?

A. Tinkerbells
B. Plays with dolls
C. Demon-possessed
D. Pre-gay

[Correct answer: D]

The Meek Shall Inherit the Earth; As Long As the Meek Aren't a Bunch of Homos

Dobson reserves the most venom for homosexuality, which he says will "destroy the earth." After all, even a dummy knows that the almighty Creator of the infinite universe spends 85 percent of his time fretting about *Will & Grace* and man-purses. Dobson believes that homosexuality is a sickness, a psychological disorder that can be cured. In the late 1990s, Dobson introduced Love Won Out as an extension of FOTF. The mission of Love Won Out was to provide "reparative therapy" to homosexuals. In other words, counseling to help them get the gay out. Ironically, the program's original director, "ex-gay" John

Paulk (who, incidentally, is married to an ex-lesbian), was scandalized in 2000 when he was spotted in a gay bar.

Not content to obsess over one issue, Dobson has chosen two, the second of course being abortion, which he has compared to the Holocaust. Dobson's trademark antiabortion program, the Option Ultrasound™ Project, equips hundreds of pregnancy centers with ultrasound equipment. His hope is to dissuade people from having abortions by showing them ultrasound pictures, if the sign-waving lunatics outside the clinics don't do the trick.

Signs of Impending Gayness in Little Boys, According to James Dobson

- "may avoid other boys in the neighborhood and their rough-and-tumble activities"
- "preference for cross-dressing, or simulating female attire"
- "strong and persistent preference for cross-sexual roles in make-believe play"
- "may start using his mother's makeup"
- "prefer[s] being with his sisters . . . who play with dolls and dollhouses."
- "may start speaking in a high-pitched voice"
- "may affect the exaggerated gestures and even the walk of a girl, or become fascinated with long hair, earrings and scarves"

Dobson on How Parents Can Help Prevent Homosexuality

"[T]he boy's father has to do his part. He needs to mirror and affirm his son's maleness. He can play rough-and-tumble games with his son, in ways that are decidedly different from the games he would play with a little girl. He can help his son learn to throw and catch a ball. He can teach him to pound a square wooden peg into a square hole in a pegboard. He can even take his son with him into the

 Quick fact: As part of their tsunami relief package, Focus on the Family distributed copies of James Dobson's book *When God Doesn't Make Sense.* (*Chicago Tribune*, 2005)

shower, where the boy cannot help but notice that Dad has a penis, just like his, only bigger."

Focus on the Legal Loophole

Dobson has become a political force by using his enormous audience to intimidate legislators. "Republicans are real good at trembling," he claims, encouraging his supporters to jam politicians' phone lines with disgruntled calls. Plus, he's been known to challenge legislators who don't back his "pro-family"[1] initiatives to fistfights after school down by the power lines. Dobson knows that when he threatens to withdraw his support, it can be fatal for Republican campaigns. After all, Focus on the Family sent out over 8 million voting guides in 2004, and Dobson made a point to tell his followers that not voting is a sin. Recently, Dobson created Focus on the Family Action, an overtly political arm of FOTF exempt from the spending limitations

Getting involved in politics is part of our calling as Christians. Jesus commissioned us to be lights in a political realm. It is the responsibility of those who claim the name of Jesus to get involved politically. Jesus was involved in the political process of the Sanhedrin . . . the true danger is if the church becomes a subculture within a particular political party.

---

[1] We've placed quotes around the term "pro-family" since the meaning of the word has been hijacked by the evangelical right. In order to avoid an eyesore, the quotes have been removed from most forthcoming instance of "pro-family" in this book. We've also removed several pro-nouns. We've decided to take an anti-noun stance since we have suspicions that the pro-noun movement is actively working to promote the homosexual agenda.

and lobbying restrictions imposed on nonprofits like FOTF. FOTF Action is essentially an extension of FOTF, only they file an income tax report, which allows them more freedom with their political contributions. Dobson can now officially endorse candidates, lobby inside the Beltway, and tongue-kiss House Speaker Dennis Hastert without losing his tax-exempt status at Focus on the Family.

James Dobson in Context

Comparing "activist judges" to the KKK: "I heard a minister the other day talking about the great injustice and evil of the men in white robes, the Ku Klux Klan, that roamed the country in the South, and they did great wrong to civil rights and to morality. And now we have black-robed men."

On the submission of wives (from Dobson's family.org Web site): "If you feel that your wife is not submissive, pray for her to have a submissive heart. . . . Then ask God to help you love her the way He does. I guarantee that you will see her submission level rise. . . ."

Evangelical 101 for the Wayward Sinner

We chose to begin with James Dobson because, well, he's scary. But he also epitomizes what most sinners think of when they hear the word "evangelical." Thankfully, as you'll see throughout this book, Dobson doesn't represent the views of all evangelicals, but his ministry provides a good peek into the extremes of the evangelical right. You're undoubtedly familiar with some evangelicals, like George W. Bush, Pat Robertson, and that distant uncle of yours who saves money by feeding his hunting dogs boiled spaghetti noodles. But to understand evangelicals and their love of pastel pantsuits with shoulder pads, you must first understand their core theological beliefs. This chapter will be a window into their culture and belief system. And it will provide information on how to get saved should the Rapture occur. You know, since none of the political or evangelical leaders discussed in this book will be left behind to explain how it all works.

The Eleven Evangelical Commandments

Thou shalt have eleven since evangelicals go that extra mile and like to supersize things.

1. Thou shalt say "have a blessed day" instead of "good-bye" to the cashier at Walgreens.
2. Thou shalt interpret "no spin zone" to mean "pillar of journalistic integrity."
3. Thou shalt live in the suburbs, eat at the Olive Garden, and wear clothes made from polyblend fabrics.
4. Thou shalt wear clean underwear at all times in preparation for the Rapture.
5. Thou shalt have a senior pastor who wears Hawaiian shirts and a youth minister with an earring.
6. Thou shalt become aware of pop culture trends eight years after the fact and co-opt these trends for Christian culture.
7. Thou shalt own a *support the troops* car magnet, a fish bumper sticker, and/or an embroidered flag sweater.
8. Thou shalt instinctively raise thy hands in praise whenever you hear Lite FM music with Christian lyrics.
9. Thou shalt believe that Harry Potter novels, Procter & Gamble, and the teenage goths who smoke clove cigarettes behind JCPenney are part of a global demonic conspiracy.
10. Thou shalt not speak ill of thy neighbor, unless thy neighbor is gay. Then it's okay.
11. Thou shalt vote Republican and encourage your local senator to change the party logo from an elephant to a fish.

Christianese

No one can truly understand the evangelical as an insider without first understanding the language they speak. We call it Christianese. Many expressions, such as the familiar "**born again**" (the spiritual rebirth Christians undergo when accepting Jesus into their lives) are taken directly from the King James Bible. Terms like the "**Rapture**"—a belief that evangelicals will supernaturally ascend into Heaven before the Antichrist takes over—are part of church interpretation of the Bible. Others terms like "**a Bible-believin' church**"—literal-minded congregations who think Noah *really* had giraffes, elephants, millipedes, and poisonous snakes on his ark—have become part of church slang.

Since evangelicals have their own distinct media and pop culture, the "Christianese" spoken in Idaho is recognizable to Christians in Texas, New York, and California. Evangelicals often reveal themselves to one another by saying things like "have a blessed day." We've provided a full glossary of Christianese at the end of this book for easy access. Familiarize yourself with these terms, and you'll be able to decode the mumbo jumbo you hear on the *700 Club*, not to mention chow on some free food at church picnics without raising suspicion.

Incidentally, George Bush regularly uses code words and phrases borrowed from Christianese to pepper his speeches. In his 2003 State of the Union address, for instance, he stated there is "power, wonder-working power, in the goodness and idealism and faith of the American people." The chorus of the staple evangelical "praise-and-worship" song "Power in the Blood" speaks of God's "power, wonder-working power."

The Core Beliefs of Evangelicals

The word "evangelical" originates from the Greek *evangelion*, which means "the good news" or "gospel." Evangelicals are "the good news people," and of course the best news is on FOX News, as is evidenced

 Quick fact: *Plugged In*, Focus on the Family's movie magazine, criticized *The 40-Year-Old Virgin* for advocating "outercourse," though we're not even sure what that means.

by the network's loyal evangelical viewership. To *evangelize* means to preach the good news—namely, by letting sinners who get their news on *The Daily Show with Jon Stewart* or NPR know that the *really good news* is on *Hannity & Colmes*. Nevertheless, evangelicals know that salvation won't come through Bill O'Reilly alone and have a more pressing agenda. They want wayward sinners to convert to their particular interpretation of the teachings of Jesus Christ. They're looking to recruit a few million wayward sinners, paganists, and Jews just like you. And though some of the particulars of being an evangelical are open to debate, here's a rundown of their core beliefs.

1. Jesus is Lord and the only son of God, though Reagan may be a distant cousin.
2. Those who develop a personal relationship with Jesus become *born-again*. Those who don't must spend an eternity in hell watching Mel Gibson's *The Passion of the Christ* over and over again with the Jews, Muslims, Hindus, and those sinners with *New York Times* subscriptions.
3. The Bible is the only *infallible* word of God, though the *Left Behind* series and Ann Coulter's *How to Talk to a Liberal* should be canonized.
4. Jesus's crucifixion and subsequent resurrection are the things that provide salvation to believers. Nevertheless, Aslan from C. S. Lewis's *Narnia* series is a metaphor for God, so if you worship him, you might get saved on a technicality.

When I come home from church carrying my Bible, people [at college] look at me like I'm crazy. They don't understand it . . . it's different here than it was in high school. It's hard to witness to people when you're, like, the only one doing it.

5. Jesus was baptized by John the Baptist and wants his believers to be baptized as well. Jesus also wore sandals, but now realizes that men who wear open-toe footwear are committing an unforgivable fashion faux pas.
6. Jesus wants his followers to evangelize the world with their kindly actions and by pressuring the local school board to adopt Intelligent Design as part of the core curriculum.

The Trinity: The Father, the Son, and Fat Bastard

Most evangelicals also believe in the *trinity*, the theological understanding that God is a schizophrenic being with three distinctive yet unified identities. Kind of like when Mike Myers played Dr. Evil, Austin Powers, and Fat Bastard all in one film. **God the Father** is the big man, the hot-tempered guy in the Old Testament who created the world and proclaims "an eye for an eye." He's the tough-guy father with the soft center, just like Dr. Evil. **Jesus** is the hippie son, written about in the New Testament, who turns water into wine and hangs out with bohemians, prostitutes, and poor people. He died to bring salvation to a bunch of undeserving welfare-state losers looking for a free salvation handout. He saves the world, just like Austin Powers. The last member of the trinity is the **Holy Spirit**. Like Fat Bastard, whose catchphrase is "get in my belly," the Holy Spirit wants to get inside *your* belly. He's the essence of God, who, according to evangelicals, *literally* lives inside them when they get born again. In addition to the trinity and the other aforementioned core beliefs, most evangelicals also believe Wal-Mart has the best savings on Crispy Wheats 'N Raisins.

Quick fact: "If it's warm and it's damp and it vibrates you might, in fact, have sex with it."

(Christian antiabortion leader Neal Horsley confessing to sex with watermelons and a mule on *The Alan Colmes Show*)

The Gifts of the Spirit

Though it seems like it might tickle, when evangelicals become born again, most believe the Holy Spirit *literally* takes up residence inside their bodies. When they say "the body is a temple," they really mean it. But when some evangelicals speak of being *spirit-filled* or *baptized in the spirit*, they're referring to an even more intimate relationship with God where the Holy Spirit fills them to overflowing, empowering them with supernatural gifts. The gifts of the Holy Spirit include faith healing, prophecy, divine "words of Knowledge," and, most commonly, the ability to speak in tongues, sometimes known as gibberish. Some evangelicals confess to having several spiritual gifts all at once. It should be noted that *being filled with the spirit* is sometimes confused with *being filled with the Hardee's biscuit*, another common attribute of many evangelicals in the heartland. Here are the other gifts of the Holy Spirit.

Common Gifts of the Holy Spirit

1. Words of Knowledge: In more fervent evangelical churches, the pastor or members of the congregation often address the church saying, "I have a Word," which means they think God wants them to relate a "Divine" anecdote to the congregation about forgiveness, overcoming sin, or who to vote for in the upcoming election. Many evangelicals use Words of Knowledge in mundane situations, saying things like "I received a Word that we should take Route 80 instead of getting on the expressway."

2. Healing: If you've seen Benny Hinn or other faith healers who exclaim "praise God, you are heeee-aaaled" before pushing little girls on crutches to the floor, you know all about this gift. At most evangelical churches, there is prayer time at the end of the service, when members "lay hands" on members who want some type of physical or spiritual healing. It's hot.

3. The Gift of Tongues: Can anyone say *boring*?! As the most common gift, receiving the gift of tongues from the Holy Spirit is like getting underwear from your granny. Evangelicals who speak in tongues have the ability, so they say, to speak the language of God. In many churches, members speak aloud in tongues during the service. Most claim that the meka-leka-hi, meka-hiney-ho dialect they're verbalizing is the language of God speaking directly through them. Sin-

I have the gift of tongues. . . . I was singing [at church] and suddenly I was singing in a language I didn't understand. I felt a rush, like hot liquid being poured all over my body. . . . I had been introduced to tongues by a group of people at a church [years before] who laid hands on me. They kept telling me to repeat what they were doing. It scared me. You shouldn't be peer pressured into it.

ners take note, you haven't truly enjoyed Chaucer, Dostoyevsky, or even Eggers until you've read them aloud in tongues. Some evangelicals say they only "pray in tongues," which simply means they do it quietly and are less obnoxious about it. Making out in tongues is usually considered to be a sin, though.

4. The Interpretation of Tongues: People who have the gift of interpretation can understand the Divine clucking of tongues. At many evangelical churches, a member will boisterously speak in tongues loud enough for everyone to hear. Then, someone with this gift will provide an interpretation, typically closing with the phrase "so sayeth the Lord." Unfortunately, the gift of interpretation doesn't bear much weight on UN applications for those trying to secure jobs as translators. And unfortunately, tongues translation dictionaries are not available yet.

5. Prophecy: Pat Robertson claims to have this self-explanatory gift. Here's his prophecy for 2006, as related on a New Year's edition of *The 700 Club:* "There will be panic and terror. . . . There will be earthquakes, tsunamis, hurricanes, tornadoes, volcanic eruption . . . this is

 Quick fact: "Four out of five people (81 percent) believe that angels exist and influence people's lives."

(Barna Group, 2000)

going to be the year when the hand of the Lord will be felt." And on Pat's Easter special, he'll be sharing some casserole recipes using the bone marrow of unrepentant deviants! It'll be a heartwarming event.

6. Teaching Abilities, Devoted Faith, and Evangelism: These are some of the more practical gifts of the Holy Spirit, akin to getting a tool box complete with a drill and multiple drill bits. Notably, the evangelicals who claim to have these less "supernatural" gifts are generally the shy or rational churchgoers who are merely sick of more zealous acquaintances who question their faith since they don't burst into tongues at PTA meetings.

Other Gifts of the Holy Spirit

1. Barnes & Noble gift certificates
2. Divine gaydar
3. Supernatural creepiness
4. Moses Chia Pets/ The Clapper
5. Heavenly casserole preparation
6. Being kick-ass at praying
7. Celestial whittling skills
8. Competitive eating
9. GOP speechwriting
10. Good at collating/Xeroxing
11. Divinely knowing in advance that you should bring a jacket because it might be chilly at Outback Steakhouse.

The Fruits of the Spirit

Some evangelicals believe the gifts of the Holy Spirit only occurred in biblical times. They think people who speak in tongues are either faking it or simply not edifying the church by using their gift publicly. This type of evangelical usually emphasizes the "fruits of the spirit," which include "Godlike" attributes such as love, patience, and kindness, that accompany a spiritual life. There has been some controversy in recent days since some Fruits of the Spirit are genetically modified and sprayed with pesticides.

Some Evangelical Statistics

Of the 70 million Americans who identify themselves as being either born-again or evangelical, 74 percent are white, 15 percent are black, and 5 percent are Hispanic. While 83 percent of all evangelicals voted for George W. Bush in 2004, the extreme right-wingers are usually white evangelicals. In fact, an estimated three out of four black evangelicals are Democrats. As a voting bloc, African-American evangelicals tend to be slightly more moderate on pro-family issues than white evangelicals and are more supportive of political candidates who are pro-labor and working to battle poverty. Unlike their Caucasian partners in faith, most African-American evangelicals also know better than to wear capris and flip-flops to the Sunday morning service. Here's a rundown of some statistics about Dubya's "base," the white evangelicals.

Statistics about White Evangelicals, As Compiled by Religion News Service

- 56 percent live in small towns or rural areas
- 79 percent believe in the Bible literally as the infallible word of God
- 85 percent oppose gay marriage, 74 percent oppose civil unions
- 67 percent think *Roe v. Wade* should be overturned
- Are 5 percent less likely than the rest of the U.S. population to hold a college degree
- 73 percent have tried to convert someone to their faith
- 84 percent think faith in Jesus is the only way to get to Heaven
- 74 percent think the mass media is hostile to their values
- 37 percent have boycotted a product or company that is in opposition to their values
- 36 percent have given money to Christian political groups or candidates
- 55 percent tune in to religious radio or watch Christian TV weekly
- Though not part of the study, white evangelicals are also 95 percent more likely to have uttered the phrase "supper's ready, come and get your chipped beef" than the rest of the population.

Twenty Celebrities Most Likely to Go to Hell, According to Evangelicals *(Ranked in Order)*

20. Ted Kennedy	**10.** Everyone on NPR
19. J. K. Rowling	**9.** Madonna
18. Dan Rather	**8.** Jon Stewart
17. Sean Penn	**7.** Elton John
16. SpongeBob SquarePants	**6.** Barbra Streisand
15. Tinky Winky	**5.** Al Franken
14. Ellen DeGeneres	**4.** Howard Dean
13. The Pope	**3.** Hillary and Bill Clinton
12. George Clooney	**2.** Osama bin Laden
11. Marilyn Manson	**1.** Michael Moore

Evangelical Church Etiquette: Visiting an Evangelical Church

Has your curiosity been piqued by all the stories about evangelicals and megachurches in the media? We recommend checking out an evangelical church as a sociological experience. You won't be struck down by lightning, though you may get a little bit sick from the secondhand hairspray fumes. It'll be an eye-opening experience. And besides, you can miss Tim Russert on *Meet the Press* this Sunday. He never asks real questions anyway. One note of caution: if you're gay, be sure to bring earplugs should the sermon be entitled "Christian Eye for the Unrepentant Deviant." Here's a rundown of how to behave and what to expect.

The Dress Code: Wear jeans. Evangelicals dress more informally because looking casual and "hip" reaps a higher conversion rate. Nevertheless, you may want to refrain from going braless in an Ozzfest tank top. The "come as you are" mantra evangelical churches promote actually means "you can have a wacky haircut, just don't act like a dirty bohemian or play the devil's music in the parking lot." If you go to an African-American evangelical church, dress a tad more formally, pick out a good hat to wear, and plan on being there until dusk.

The Props: Don't bring the King James Bible. That's for college lit professors and other sinners. Evangelicals'prefer the New International Version (NIV). To avoid being conspicuous, your Bible should be worn from multiple readings and be filled with margin notes. Preferably bring a copy of the *Left Behind* series and *Guideposts* magazine to the service as well. At megachurches, regular congregants often arrive early and save their seats with their Bibles. And be sure to leave your cigarettes at home, since evangelicals only like *lawmakers* who support the tobacco industry.

Getting There: If you're attending a megachurch, leave extra time for traffic jams. Starbucks will be available in the lobby right next to the petting zoo, which saves time. Cover your subversive *Think Globally, Act Locally* bumper sticker with the more evangelical-friendly substitution: *Think Heavenly, the Environmentalists Shall Burn in Godless Iniquity.*

Talk the Talk: When making small talk with evangelicals before the service, refrain from saying, "Man, I am so hungover" and "Do any hot Bible-thumper chicks go here?" Make a point to end your phrases with "in accordance with prophecy" or "so sayeth the Lord" to lend yourself spiritual credibility. Find out in advance if the church's preferred term for the devil is "Satan," "the beast," "Lucifer," or "Clinton." Familiarize yourself with Christian buzzwords like "bless-ed," "filled with the spirit," "prayer warrior," and "Halliburton." When congregants boast that they boycotted *The Da Vinci Code*, distinguish yourself by saying you boycotted *The Passion of the Christ* since Mel Gibson is Catholic and was in other godless movies like *Lethal Weapon.*

During the Service: Raise your hands in the air when others do. Not doing so is a faux pas. Holding a lit Zippo above your head may be frowned upon, though. If someone begins contorting and making strange noises, don't perform the Heimlich. He or she is probably speaking in tongues. Saying "Amen," "Hallelujah," "Glory," or "Preach it" are socially acceptable ways to vocalize your enthusiasm during the sermon. Nevertheless, vocalizing your approval with an animated "fuck yeah" is not recommended.

 Quick fact: The debate team at Jerry Falwell's fundamentalist Baptist college, Liberty University, was ranked number one in the country in 2006, outranking Ivy League schools like Harvard and Princeton   *(Newsweek, 2006)*

The Offering: Not giving money can raise suspicion. If you don't want to give when the plate comes by, tell your neighbor you do direct deposit. Or better yet, tell them you give to another ministry, the Republican National Committee.

Leaving: At the end of the service, free food and church insignia key chains will be available for newcomers. There's always a couple of bright-eyed church greeters who've been married since they were sixteen blocking the path to the 'Nilla Wafers and Kool-Aid. They'll want to hug you, look deeply into your eyes, and lay their hands on you—which are riddled with paper cuts from intense Bible study. The thirty minutes of weepy prayer that follow are not worth the wafers.

Moderate praise   Moved by the Spirit   Jesus-induced
convulsions

Pick a Tribe: Evangelical Denominations

In addition to categorizing people as "going to hell" and "not going to hell," evangelicals have formed distinctive tribes among themselves known as denominations. For sinners with a little knowledge, denominations are a great way to discern which churches to avoid should you be invited to a Christmas mass. Sadly, the politically moderate "mainline" denominations—the ones with hymnals who've been rethinking their discriminatory stance on gays—have been undergoing a steady decline since the sixties. Meanwhile, ultraconservative Baptists, Pentecostals, and churches with gun racks in their pews continue to grow. They call themselves "Bible-believin'" and often blame the decline of mainline churches on sin. (Mainline churches have come under attack by conservative groups; see the Institute on Religion and Democracy on p. 174.)

Ironically, the conservative denominations are the most cutting-edge these days. They use drums, have DJ Sin-Eclipse on the turntables, and hire pastors who feel comfortable using the word "dude" from the pulpit. Needless to say, these innovations really bring in the numbers. Meanwhile, the mainline denominations—Methodists, Episcopalians, Lutherans, Presbyterians, and Congregationalists—stagnate in outdated traditions, singing stale renditions of "Holy, Holy, Holy" while Fanny, the church librarian, plays organ accompaniment.

In the past, denominations defined themselves around profound theological doctrinal beliefs, like whether to sprinkle or dunk when baptizing. But defining denominations today is a murky task. Many have broken with their traditions and become "spirit-filled," "reformed," and/or "more creepy than your granny's church." That said, here's a breakdown of some of the biggest branches of Evangelicalism.

I don't really like calling myself an evangelical. I'm not fond of categories. I prefer being called a follower of Christ. . . . I also think a lot of damage gets done through denominational warfare. Can't we just figure out that we're all on the same team?

The Conservative Evangelical Denominations

Pentecostals and Charismatics: The fastest-growing branch of Christianity, which includes many denominations, such as the popular Assembly of God. These are the "spirit-filled" ones who speak in tongues, hear voices, TiVo Benny Hinn, and think the graffiti on the building down by the old creek is the work of a demonic coven. Pentecostal and Charismatic churches all have a resident born-again Deadhead who used to work at a headshop named Scarlet Begonias until life became meaningless when Jerry Garcia died. In backwoods towns, it's the Pentecostals who are known for burning records and handling snakes, the latter being a religious ritual we wish Falwell would warm up to.

 Most of the gifts of the Holy Spirit that Pentecostals speak of, like tongues, aren't attainable anymore. That only happened in Old Testament times. I've been to Pentecostal churches where they speak in tongues . . . it kind of freaked me out.

Nondenominational: The common choice for yuppie boomers who raise their hands in the air and brag that their church is hip because their pastor sprinkles his sermons with anecdotes from *Dr. Quinn, Medicine Woman*. Boomers are flaky, which is why they can't even make up their minds about which denomination they want to subscribe to. These *non*denominations are in denial about being independent, since the vast majority of them subscribe to the same homogenous set of conservative politics and biblical literalism. Nevertheless, their pastors are liberal when it comes to the collection plate. Money is money, and they know it would be prejudice to call the offering Baptist, Methodist, or Presbyterian.

Baptists: Believed to be the inbred stepchild of the Amish, the Baptist denomination is still synonymous with literal interpretations of the Bible, fried chicken, and deacons with names like Slim and Earl. Each church is self-governed—which explains their antigovernment rugged individualism and dislike of men who windsurf—though most belong to the Southern Baptist Convention. Ironically, a belief in separation of church and state was one of their founding principles, but the denomination has become even more conservative recently, with leaders who think a Nativity Scene would look great next to the Lincoln Memorial. Billy Graham, Rick Warren, and Jerry Falwell are Baptists, and it's the largest denomination in the United States, with more adherents than Catholicism. With the exception of some African-American churches, most Baptists think *liberalism* is a sexually transmitted disease. In the old days, many Baptists forbade dancing, until Kevin Bacon came along and starred in the inspirational religious film *Footloose*.

The Moderate Evangelical Denominations

Methodists (The United Methodist Church): Followers of John Wesley, who encouraged people to use reason to understand the gist of the Bible, as opposed to just assuming talking snakes actually existed in the Garden of Eden. Unlike Baptists, they submit to a hierarchal governing structure and don't use as much mayo in their potato salad. Relatively speaking, they're somewhat progressive. On abortion, for instance, they claim to be "equally bound to respect the sacredness of the life and well-being of the mother." There has been lots of debate within the church about their stance on gays. Nevertheless, George W. Bush is a Methodist, and he's stickin' to his guns about them gays being a buncha queers.

Presbyterians (Presbyterian Church USA): Like Methodists, only with more committee meetings and potluck dinners. Most are politically moderate, despite their backward Calvinist roots, which support the doctrine of "The Elected," the free will–defying belief that some are predestined to go to Heaven, while everyone else is doomed to hell. Most today simply think The Elected would be a kick-ass name for a Christian praise-and-worship band. The Presbyterians encourage "an atmosphere of open debate" on the abortion issue, and some churches have even ordained homosexuals. Ronald Reagan was a Presbyterian.

Congregationalists: Popular among backsliding Yankee intellectuals who only go to church during "the Holidays." Not to mention

 Quick fact: A partial list of companies who have pulled ads due to pressure and boycotts by the American Family Association since 2004: Procter & Gamble, Safeway, Tyson Foods, Liberty Mutual, Kohl's, Lowe's, Lenscrafters, RadioShack, Papa John's, Sharpie, Foot Locker, Geico, Finish Line, Best Buy, Nissan, Goodyear, Castrol, and Kraft.

(L.A. Weekly, 2005)

their concerned, *Reader's Digest*–reading grannies, who are always praying their city-slicker relatives will see the light.

The Sinful Branches

Catholics: They've got that whole pope thing and too much bureaucracy for flag-wavin', freedom-lovin' evangelicals. Evangelicals emphasize a *personal* relationship with Jesus that doesn't have to go through a priest. Besides, Catholics don't have any good Contemporary Christian bands like Creed, Plankeye, or Switchfoot.

Lutherans and Episcopalians: Too many candles and vestments. Evangelicals prefer waterslides and big screens. Plus, Episcopalians are the most likely denomination to have an openly gay choir director, as opposed to the closeted gay one at the local Bible Church.

Quakers and Unitarian Universalists: Quakers are more concerned with helping the poor, reading *The Tao of Pooh*, and tending their macrobiotic gardens than evangelizing.

Universalists think everyone will be saved, which is particularly troublesome to evangelicals and Christians who dig the Bible's sadistic stuff.

What about Fundamentalists?

That's not a denomination. It just means you believe the Bible is literally true, avoid stuff like alcohol and R-rated movies, and say "you're wrong, because the Bible says so" a lot. If the Bible were to describe a *fork* in the road, fundamentalists would miss the metaphor and think God was referring to a utensil you can eat Vienna sausages with.

The Word of God

The Rapture Must Have Gotten Raptured Out of the Bible

Evangelicals consider the Bible, along with those witty columns by Dave Barry, to be the infallible word of God. But most show little interest in the historical context of the sixty-six books that make up the Protestant Bible. Instead, most evangelicals prefer to remove scriptures from their context and card-catalog them by topic, such as marriage, the Creation, and trickle-down economics. This is known as *systematic theology* and it helps evangelicals understand what the Bible has to say on important topics like poverty, sin, and that important question, *Is Dr. Phil saved?* The problem is that systematic theology ignores the Bible's history. There is no section of the Bible, for instance, devoted to the Rapture. In fact, the term is never mentioned. But with systematic theology, scholars were able to throw several unconnected scriptures into a bowl, sprinkle on a little nutmeg, eye-o'-newt, and boom, the belief of magic escalators to Heaven was forged. Systematic theology created the Rapture.

Jesus Went Back to Heaven and All I Got Was This Crappy Bible

Most people assume the New Testament was written by Jesus's disciples, the people who, excluding Pat Robertson, possess the most knowledge about Jesus's life. In truth, most scholars believe the stories of Jesus circulated as oral traditions for over sixty-five years before being written down. Kind of like the childhood game, telephone, where a whispered phrase like "I love kittens" becomes transformed into "sulfuric fires eternally burning flesh." Most believe John is the least accurate Gospel. It's estimated to have been written nearly a century after the events it describes and paints a very different picture of Jesus than the other three Gospels. Whereas in the other Gospels—Matthew, Mark, and Luke—Jesus repeatedly instructed his disciples to avoid telling people he was the Messiah (known as "the messianic secret"), the Gospel of John is filled from start to finish with all those *follow Jesus or burn* passages popular with fundamentalists. Predictably, John is the most quoted Gospel with most evangelicals. Most even prefer the Gospel of John to Larry the Cable Guy's book *Git-R-Done*.

Lost in Translation

It certainly takes faith to believe that the Gospels, which were written about two thousand years ago by guys who ate locusts, are literally true. But given that most evangelicals are able to believe the GOP talking points written by Bush's advisors (incidentally, Karl Rove enjoys an occasional locust as well), we suppose that, by comparison, trusting the infallibility of the Bible is hardly an enormous leap of faith. Nevertheless, much of the context of the Bible was lost when it was translated from its original Greek, Hebrew, and Aramaic. A conspicuous example is the translation of the term "holy spirit" or "holy ghost," which originally meant "God's breath." Today, this profound concept has been translated in most Bibles to represent some strange approximation of Casper the Evangelical Ghost. And most notably, the term "Son of God"—often attributed to Jesus to demonstrate his kinship to the Big Man—was commonly used in Jesus's day to mean someone who was righteous. According to the Jewish Encyclopedia, "the term by no means carries the idea of physical descent from, and essential unity with, God the Father . . . [Son of God] conveys nothing further than a simple expression of godlikeness."

King James, Text Message Bibles, and the New International Version

Your grandma's Bible probably said King James on the cover, but today there are too many Bible translations to count. From the New Revised Standard Version to the New Living Translation, the choices are endless. Today, an MP3 Bible is even available for download to your iPod. Even more bizarre, an Australian company known as the Bible Society is offering a text message translation of the Good News called the SMS Bible. Now Genesis 1:1 can be read directly on your cellphone screen and is translated as "In da Bginnin God cre8d da heavens & da earth." Other translations include:

- 1 John 4:19: "We luv coz God luvd us 1st."
- Exodus 20:12: "Respect ur father & ur mother, & u will live a long time in da l& I am givin u."

 Quick fact: To solidify their support of Intelligent Design, the Kansas Board of Education recently changed the official statewide definition of the word "science" to account for the possibility of supernatural explanations.

(New York Times, 2005)

- Genesis 1:2: "Da earth waz barren, wit no 4m of life; it waz unda a roaring ocean cuvred wit dRkness."

Among evangelicals, the New International Version, called the NIV by hep evangelicals in the know, is hands down the most popular and bestselling translation for today's "Bible-believin'" Christian. It was specifically translated by a committee to appeal to the predominant beliefs of conservative evangelicals, though the tear-out GOP-stamped voter registration cards were likely omitted at the last minute.

Still, the publishers of the NIV have been in hot water following the recent release of Today's New International Version (TNIV). The translation, which was their attempt to branch out to a younger crowd, sparked a huge controversy for its "feminist" decision to include gender-neutral pronouns. The translation was especially controversial with fundamentalist men who got beat up by girls behind the jungle gym in elementary school. Compare for yourself:

ISAIAH 19:16
New International Version: "In that day Egyptians will be like women. . . ."
Today's New International Version: "In that day Egyptians will become weaklings. . . ."

MARK 1:17
New International Version: "I will make you fishers of Men."
Today's New International Version: "I will send you out to fish for people."

EPHESIANS 5:22–23
New International Version: "[22] Wives, submit to your husbands as to the Lord. [23] For the husband is the head of the wife as Christ is the head of the church. . . ."
Today's *Even Newer Secular Elitist* International Version: "[22] Wives, submit thyself to the sofa tonight. [23] For your do-nothing husband is the head of kitchen and shalt cook you dinner since it's his turn. . . ."

Recently, the NIV even released military versions of the Bible for the troops in Iraq. They have camouflage covers, feature military branch insignia, and even include "maps with overlays of ancient Mesopotamia and the modern-day Middle East." Soldiers can see first-hand where ancient Babylon is in relation to the Garden of Eden, Nazareth, Abu Ghraib, and the Saudi-owned oil fields. Over 400,000 of these camouflage-cover Bibles have been handed out to the troops by the producers of the NIV, the International Bible Society.

The Creation Museum teaches that humans and dinosaurs coexisted.

HOLY SH!T

The Creation Museum and the Jurassic Bait & Switch

"Imagine soaring cypress trees, the sounds of waterfalls and children playing with dinosaurs," reads the Creation Museum's promotional material. It's not a fantasy, they insist. The earth is only six thousand years old, was created in six twenty-four-hour days, and there *really* was a time when children played fetch with stegosauruses. Just like in *The Flintstones*! At least that's what you'll learn at this $25 million institute, due to open soon in Petersburg, Kentucky. As reported by *Esquire*, a recent sneak-peek tour for "charter members" even revealed a large dinosaur model fitted with a riding saddle.

The Creation Museum is being built by Answers in Genesis USA, a group of "scientists" who base their understanding of the earth's development on the book of Genesis. These "Young Earth Creationists" teach that baby dinosaurs rode with Noah and his family on an ark for 371 days while the rest of creation drowned in a flood. Their literature also explains that all beasts, including T. Rex and lions, were vegetarians until Eve ate the apple in the Garden of Eden. They also insist that all of humanity descended from Noah—since everyone else died in the biblical Flood—meaning that all races have developed their own physical traits in a matter of a few generations.

In addition to the Creation Museum, several "young earth" museums are already operating in the United States. In fact, there are a handful of giant roadside dinosaur attractions that pull a bait-and-switch of Jurassic proportions; they're actually evangelical outreaches promoting the belief that dinosaurs and humans coexisted. The roadside dinosaur park in Cabazon, California (featured in *Pee-wee's Big Adventure*), was recently bought by evangelicals. They use the park to proselytize and distribute literature debunking evolution.

The blingtastic Creflo Dollar and Joel Osteen

2

Joel Osteen and Our Prosperity-Lovin' Megachurch Nation

Joel Osteen: The Evangelical P. Diddy

Fire and Brimstone Score: 4
Denomination: Nondenominational charismatic/Pentecostal church
Nutshell: Evangelical self-help guru whose Houston-based megachurch meets in the former home of the Houston Rockets
Born: 1963
Defining Quote: "We obviously are a business because we're dealing with millions of dollars."

Quick Facts about the "Smiling Pastor," Joel Osteen
- Pastors the largest megachurch in the United States.
- Author of the bestselling book, *Your Best Life Now: 7 Steps to Living at Your Full Potential*
- His television broadcast can be seen in 100 million households in the United States.
- His speaking tour recently sold out two nights at Madison Square Garden.
- Believes literally in Noah's ark and says his mom was healed of cancer by Jesus.
- Has a team of interns who dab his ever-smiling teeth and gums with a wet towel when they become overly dry.

The Evangelical P. Diddy: King of the Megachurch

Think a career as a lawyer or doctor is lucrative? Become a tele-vangelist and avoid the schooling. Oral Roberts University dropout Joel Osteen is already so rich he's agreed to waive his six-figure pastor's salary and vows to never ask for donations from his millions of TV viewers. He's the toothy young pastor of the largest congregation in the nation, Lakewood Church in Houston, Texas. They meet in the former home of the Houston Rockets and actually manage to fill it twice each Sunday morning. Mr. Osteen's upbeat, condemnation-free messages—not to mention Lakewood's arcade, complete with thirty-two video games—focus on injecting the *fun* into FUNdamentalism. Plus, Lakewood Church is always guaranteed to have the most spirit-filled traffic jams in town!

Osteen's message is a crowd pleaser. He preaches that devoted Christians will receive a little bling bling from God. After all, *Osteen's* devoted, and look at him. He's got a $75 million church, not to mention a $100 million smile just begging for a few gold teeth. Osteen may not be street, like P. Diddy, but if you buy into his belief that Christians are meant to prosper, he's definitely keeping it real. Joel Osteen is the king of evangelical culture's shining, gigantic, gaudy achievement. No, we're not talking about Creed. Joel Osteen is the king of the megachurch.

Who's Your Daddy?

Joel Osteen was born in Houston, the oldest son of John Osteen, from whom he inherited his multiracial Lakewood congregation. His father was expelled from his own Baptist church in the '50s for speaking in tongues and decided to start up his own congregation in an abandoned feed store in Lakewood. Unsure if he could fill his father's shoes, Joel literally wore a pair of John's loafers while preaching his

---

 Quick fact: In Waynesville, North Carolina, Baptist pastor Chan Chandler kicked nine congregants out of his church for supporting John Kerry in 2004. He resigned after it became a national scandal. *(Charlotte Observer, 2006)*

early sermons. Frightening wardrobe habits aside, the church has grown from six thousand to thirty thousand since he took over in 1999 as senior pastor. Always loyal to his family, Osteen commonly reminisces lovingly about his father in interviews, referring to him as "Daddy"—a radical move, since most of his congregation undoubtedly prefers the more Texan-sounding "Diddy."

From Rags to Waterfalls

In July 2005, Osteen's rapidly expanding Lakewood Church moved into the Compaq Center, the former home of the Houston Rockets. Nevertheless, Osteen's congregation has already outgrown the arena. They require five weekly services to pack everyone in. Lakewood takes in so much cash, the church has its own vault to store the offering, not to mention their parking lot has enough American flag bumper stickers to employ several dozen sweatshops in China. Given that Osteen's preaching is akin to a less dynamic Tony Robbins, spectacle seems to be Lakewood's biggest draw. As one congregant recently told the *New York Times*, "With the waterfalls [which are on either side of the stage] this really feels like a sanctuary."

Quick Facts about Lakewood Megachurch

- Renovations cost $92 million.
- Has two working waterfalls, a state-of-the-art hydraulic stage, an Internet café, and three hundred employees.
- Features an adjacent five-story building with its own restaurant and a view of downtown Houston.
- Thirty thousand worshippers attend every week. Special events have drawn sixty thousand.
- They sell discount bulk food on the premises, like a Jesusy Sam's Club.
- Joel's enormous teeth projected to fifty times their natural height on Lakewood's multiple screens undoubtedly scare the hell out of hundreds of children each Sunday.

The Smiling Pastor

Osteen begins his upbeat sermons by telling his audience in his thick Texan twang, "You're looking good" or "You sound great." Part of a growing trend among many young pastors, Osteen avoids talking about sin at all. He doesn't want to turn people (or tithes) off. "I think for years there's been a lot of hellfire and damnation," Osteen told FOX News. "We believe in focusing on the goodness of God." Osteen's big grin and happy demeanor—uh, he's worth millions—have earned him the nickname "the smiling pastor." Still, that guy who pastors the wimpy start-up church down the street calls him "the grinning douchebag."

Many evangelical critics refer to Osteen's prosperity-promising, condemnation-free, motivational sermons as "Christian-Lite." His sermons—which have titles like "The Dangers of Procrastination" and "Have the Courage to Be Different"—are often more akin to self-help conferences than fire-and-brimstone tent revivals. In a recent interview on *Larry King Live*, Osteen said: "I don't have it in my heart to condemn people," voicing apparent uncertainty about whether Jesus was the sole way to achieve salvation. Playing both sides of the fence, he later apologized on his Web site for not making it clear that he believed Muslims and Buddhists would burn in godless iniquity alongside, presumably, Larry King.

Is He Political?

Osteen has never been overtly political, but he does toe the Republican faith-based, family values, antigay, antichoice party line. Like his compatriot in fame, Rick Warren (p. 53), he's a cultural conservative who distances himself from the political limelight to avoid polarizing people. With regard to hot-button issues, Osteen routinely states, in his folksy aw-shucks manner, that he "doesn't go there." When asked

My heart goes out to a mother who has an unwanted pregnancy. I don't call abortion a sin. I call it a tragedy. . . . [Abortion] lacks compassion and the heart of Christ, but we need to learn how to communicate in a much more compassionate way about this issue as a church.

about abortion, for instance, he's said, "I don't know the answers." Nevertheless, representatives from his office at Lakewood confirm that the church is "definitely pro-family, and pro-life." And in regard to gay rights, Osteen has gone on record saying: "I don't think that a same-sex marriage is the way God intended it to be." Still, he apparently holds firm to his convictions that God is a huge proponent of churches with waterfalls and Ms. Pac-Man.

QUICK QUIZ: Which of the following credit cards are accepted at Lakewood for tithes and offerings?

A. Visa
B. MasterCard
C. American Express
D. Discover
E. All of the above

[Correct answer: E]

The Prosperity Gospel: Jesus Loves a Little Bling

Osteen is the bling-tastic patron saint of what is known as the prosperity gospel. He teaches that being a faithful evangelical—which includes tithing 10 percent of your income to the church—provides much more than some pansy run-of-the-mill salvation. Being a faithful, money-giving evangelical ensures a large return on your investment—namely, God will bless your devotion with a Range

---

 Quick fact: In 2004, the *Washington Times* owner (and ultraconservative) Sun Myung Moon was crowned by Senator Danny Davis of Illinois in a bizarre coronation ceremony. Adorned in the jeweled crown, Moon declared himself "savior" and "Messiah." The event took place in a Senate building and several congressmen were in attendance.

(*The Hill*, 2004)

Rover, an elegant mansion by the bay, and a flat-panel high-definition TV with Sony surround-sound speakers. "God wants to bless you," says Osteen. About the only thing the prosperity gospel doesn't promise are hos and bitches. Of course, the implications of Osteen's prosperity gospel are disturbing: if you're poor, there's something spiritually wrong with you. Even Ole Anthony, an evangelical minister who investigates fraud in churches, has doubts about Osteen's ministry. "What about helping the poor in society?" he asks in an article published by the *Boston Globe*. "Houston has thousands of homeless people. What is [Osteen] doing for them?"

Controversy aside, Osteen seems to be a savvy businessman. He's learned from disgraced prosperity gospel preachers like Jim Bakker, who focused almost entirely on money. He preaches a more expansive form of prosperity gospel that promises psychological well-being in addition to money. Plus, he's been blessed with a wife who wears a tad less mascara than Tammy Faye. All the same, even some ultra-conservatives like the National Association of Evangelicals' Ted Haggard call the prosperity gospel "heretical." After all, the prosperity gospel is often referred to as "name-it-and-claim-it," since many of its adherents believe that God will simply give them whatever they ask for if they are devoted with their tithes. Especially if they ask for credit card debt!

Just because someone is a pastor, does that mean they have to drive around in a Grand Am instead of a Rolls-Royce? The easy thing to do would be to not drive the Rolls to avoid the criticism. Me personally, I don't need a nice car, but there are a lot more scriptures saying God wants Christians to be wealthy than scriptures that say He wants them to be poor.

The Prosperity of Joel Osteen's *Your Best Life Now*

"Think big. Think increase. Think abundance. Think more than enough," Osteen instructs in the first chapter of his hugely popular book, *Your Best Life Now*. Its opening anecdote tells of a man distraught because he can't afford a mansion in Hawaii. Osteen asserts that if he wants to own that mansion, he must *"enlarge [his] vision."* Believers who "conceive and believe," Osteen writes, will receive God's "preferential treatment" because "God wants to increase you financially." Osteen's conceivin' and believin' has evidently served him well. He's a mansion owner. His home in Tanglewood, Texas, was appraised at $2.3 million. And *Your Best Life Now* is one of the bestselling books in recent history. It did so well, Osteen's publisher provided him with a private jet for his book tour. Surprisingly, its less positive predecessor, *God: He's Just Not That into You*, never found its market.

Discarded Joel Osteen Book Titles
• Get Rich or Die Prayin'
• The Master's Card: Charging Toward Heaven
• The One Facial Expression of Highly Effective People
• Faith on Deposit
• It Takes a Basketball Arena
• Fluoride Treatment
• The Dummy's Guide to Their Wallets

- A Smile is Worth a Thousand Tithe Commitments
- The Purpose Driven Grin

Jesus Really Loves Osteen

Osteen believes that devoted Christians can even receive Divine favor in mundane affairs, like getting seated quickly at Red Lobster, encountering light traffic on the way to Kohl's, or presumably getting the high score on Pac-Man in the Lakewood Church arcade. As reported in *Christianity Today*, Osteen writes in *Best Life Now* that he was able to convince an airplane pilot to stow his TV camera in the cockpit, despite having been informed by the counter clerk that the camera needed to be checked with the rest of his luggage:

> *"The woman behind the counter glared at me and shook her head, clearly aggravated. I just smiled and said, 'Sorry, ma'am; it's the favor of God.'"*

Praise God! Pick up a copy of *Your Best Life Now* today and *you too* can Divinely irritate low-wage workers trying to do their jobs. The Osteens apparently have a long history of annoying flight attendants. They were recently kicked off a flight for arguing with a flight attendant for failing to follow the airline's rules.

"Think More Than Enough"

Lakewood Church may soon be coming to a former basketball arena near you. Osteen and his staff often discuss their desire to continue growing as a church. "I can see us having [a] Lakewood Philadelphia, Lakewood Atlanta, Lakewood Detroit," Lakewood's executive director, Duncan Dodds, told *Texas Monthly*. "I see the opportunity to expand this ministry," he continued, "and almost franchise it." Pass the sweet-'n'-sour sauce. Them McOsteen Nuggets is Yum-Mee.

Osteen in Context

On His Fortune: "Roger Clemens just signed for $18 million—man, don't tell me I can't have a nice house and send my kids to college."

On Prosperity: "Even if you come from an extremely successful family, God still wants you to go further."

Our Prosperity-Lovin' Megachurch Nation

Megachurches: serving millions

"These are not just churches; they are also corporations."
Scott Thumma, Megachurch Expert at the Hartford Institute

The Redcoats Are Coming

The little corner church that your grandparents attended is dying. According to a recent study published in the book *Breakout Churches:*

Quick fact: "In general, higher rates of belief in and worship of a creator correlate with higher rates of homicide, juvenile and early adult mortality, STD infection rates, teen pregnancy and abortion in the prosperous democracies."

(Journal of Religion and Society, 2005)

Discover How to Make the Leap, church membership is on the decline in 80 percent of the nation's churches. Curiously, the country seems more religious than it's ever been. Those Jesus-fish stickers seem to be on the bumper of every SUV at the A&P. And we wouldn't be surprised if the next round of political campaign commercials featured patriotic imagery of candidates burning their old album collections in front of the Washington Monument.

Though overall church attendance has been on the decline for decades, lately it's been the moderate, mainline churches (Presbyterians, Episcopalians, Methodists, Lutherans) that have taken the brunt of the beating. Meanwhile, the attendance rates at the Bush-lovin' "spirit-filled" churches—you know, the ones with drums instead of organs that hide the snake cages beneath American flags—have been on the rise. The growing dominance of conservative churches has sinners and blue-staters yelling, "The Redcoats are coming!" Though in truth, most evangelicals are more likely to be wearing *Redskins* and/or other NFL franchise jackets and think most of the Brits are a bunch of secular elitists.

Megachurches are run like corporations. They want people to leave feeling good so they'll come back. In the process, they water down the scripture.

The Monster Truck Churches

As the cultural impact of Joel Osteen illustrates, we're living in the era of the megachurch, enormous, exurban, sprawling churches that architecturally have more in common with a mall than a traditional church. Though they only represent a small percentage of the churches in the United States, state-of-the-art megachurches have raised the bar for what to expect from a church. After all, who wants to go to some pussy plywood building with a steeple and potluck dinners? Megachurches have laser tag and Big Macs. They're the one-stop, praise-'til-you-drop, we-got-it-all supercenters of evangelicaldom. Mainline

A lot of my friends are joining smaller churches or having services out of their homes. There's no community in these huge churches. That's the point of them, to be anonymous, which isn't what church is about.

church is for old people and pansies. Megachurches have better music, better food courts, and stuff to do every night of the week. And though attendance at the politically moderate mainline churches was on the decline before the megachurch phenomenon took root, megachurch culture is shoveling the final dirt onto their hymnal-filled casket. Just like on Capitol Hill, the clueless moderates are getting their asses beat by the ever-more-resourceful conservatives.

Quick Facts: Megachurches[1]
- Megachurches have a minimum of two thousand members, though several have in excess of twenty thousand.

I currently head up the Backwards Messaging small group at my church. On Saturdays, we get together to crank out the classics at full blast. If the weather's nice, we'll bleed a goat or a stray dog. I also oversee the church bake sale. Next time you're in town, you simply *must* try our blood muffins.

---

[1] Numerical statistics from the Hartford Institute for Religion Research, 2006

- There are over twelve hundred megachurches in the United States, a number that has nearly doubled since 2000.
- Most megachurch pastors have wives who wear blouses with shoulder pads.
- They primarily attract college-educated, suburban, middle-class baby boomers who regularly eat at Applebee's.
- 83 percent are ultraconservative, politically and culturally.
- The average yearly income of a megachurch is $6 million.
- California has the most megachurches of any state, 178.
- Some have started referring to larger ones as gigachurches, but we don't want to encourage them.

The Rise of the Megachurch: Jesus Loves Micro-dermabrasion

Given the declines in attendance, churches today are eager to please. West End Assembly of God in Richmond, Virginia, hosts Broadway-style musicals with live camels and flying angels dangling from the ceilings. Radiant Church in Arizona keeps the baptismal pool heated to 101 degrees. "It's like taking a dip in a spa," their pastor told the *New York Times*. Willow Creek Community Church in Illinois offers free haircuts, facials, micro-dermabrasion, massages, manicures, and makeup application via an outreach program operated by Christian beauty specialists. And New Life Church in Colorado Springs attracted thousands of visitors last Halloween by placing high-flying trampolines just outside their entranceway. The site of children flying through the air no doubt concerned some churchgoers that the Rapture had perhaps left them behind.

The Largest Protestant Megachurches in the Country[2]

Megachurch	Pastor	Attendees
Lakewood Church, Houston, Texas	Joel Osteen	30,000
The Potter's House, Dallas, Texas	T. D. Jakes	28,000

[2] These are estimates, since many megachurches tend to inflate their attendance numbers, a very ungodly thing to do.

World Changers, College Park, Georgia	Creflo Dollar	25,000
Saddleback Valley Community Church, Lake Forest, California	Rick Warren	22,000
Calvary Chapel of Costa Mesa, Santa Ana, California	Chuck Smith	20,000
Willow Creek Community Church, Illinois	Bill Hybels	20,000

The Jesus Freaks: Dirty Hippies Spearhead a Movement

Though rarely credited for their contribution, mainly because they smell like dirty hippies, the Jesus Freaks of the late sixties and early seventies were partially responsible for the reform of the Protestant Church that paved the way for the modern megachurch. The Jesus Freaks (sometimes known as the Jesus People, or simply the tick-infested, pinko, commie Bible-thumpers) were born-again hippies who did way too many drugs before realizing their dreamcatchers and Ouija boards were tools of the Beast. Instead of protesting 'Nam, they protested wearing ties on Sunday morning and set in motion a movement to make church more casual, more Pentecostal, and more ripe with the smell of B.O. Most notably, they introduced the church to the Devil's music, which has now come to be known as Contemporary Christian Rock, the bedrock of the megachurch. The Jesus Freaks were embraced by the pastor of California's Calvary Chapel Costa Mesa, Chuck Smith, who added some Haight-Ashbury longhairs to his staff to attract the Jesus Freak crowd. The move got national attention and spearheaded a movement. Today, Smith's Calvary Chapel has over a thousand loosely affiliated churches worldwide. Despite their hippie roots, it's next to impossible to get any weed at any of the Calvary Chapel churches. Predictably, most of the evangelical hippies became yuppies.

Megachurches Are MegaFun!

Megachurches attract crowds by delivering spectacle. Megachurch worship services generally incorporate full bands, professional lighting, and state-of the-art video projections of gleeful children with bowl cuts running through heavenly fields of wheat. Hand lifting, swaying, clapping, and even jumping during "praise and worship" is encouraged. Pressing, copping, and grinding, on the other hand, are generally frowned upon. Though churches with ATMs, free Internet, and Whack-a-Mole may seem bizarre to the uninitiated sinner, its makes sense that a consumer-driven culture would expect more from its houses of worship than mere salvation. According to a Hartford Institute for Religion Research report on megachurches, there are a variety of reasons megachurches have become popular. We'll put the gist of the study in layman's terms and note some of the draws we've noticed as well.

Why Megachurches Have Become So Popular

Everyone's doing it: People want to see what all the commotion is about. It's pack mentality. The size of a megachurch is its best recruitment tool.

The Wal-Mart school of architectural design: Evangelicals feel comfy in megachurches because they resemble the places they work, go to school, and buy their Cheez Whiz. Typical megachurches are designed to look like large generic spaces that resemble office parks and malls. Knowing it could turn off the "unchurched," megachurches usually avoid overtly Christian iconography like stained glass, crucifixes, and images of flag-waving soldiers kicking towelhead ass.

You won't be a nervous Nillie: If you're visiting a church the size of Rhode Island, chances are you won't be singled out, a big draw for new visitors. After all, first thing in the morning, nobody wants to talk to some evangelical you barely know about getting involved in the latest Procter & Gamble boycott. Especially when you're trying to *get your praise on* listening to DJ Sin-Eclipse.

They're relevant: Megachurches attract younger churchgoers because they don't have "that old person smell" you encounter at your granny's Church of the Redeemed Heart. Plus, the dress is casual. Ser-

 Quick fact: Wal-Mart is the world's largest retailer of Christian products. *(Forbes* magazine, 2004)

mons are often about current issues. And the music rocks hard, like on *American Idol*. Nevertheless, since tradition is important to evangelicals, most megachurch pastors still include a joke or two every Sunday about how women gossip, shop, and/or nag too much.

Kids are annoying: Megachurches cater to busy schedules with countless services, activities, and even child care throughout the week, so you can drop the little demons off and get some peace and quiet.

More hotties to choose from in a big church: Oddly, the Hartford Institute for Religion didn't mention this essential truth.

Praise Aerobics and small groups: Most megachurches strongly encourage people to join a small group—which often meet in people's homes—to strengthen bonds to the church. New Life Church in Colorado Springs has an estimated fifteen thousand church-affiliated small groups, including Praise Aerobics, Worship Hula, Biblical Creationism vs. Evolution, Volleyball with James (where you play volleyball as a warm-up to studying the book of James), and our favorite, an arts group called Mom & Me Rubber-Stamping. Some megachurches hire Ministers of Pain to beat unruly congregants down should they fail to join one. Small groups take advantage of Christianity's best conversion tool: peer pressure.

Christian "cocooning": Megachurches provide a wholesome alternative culture, separate from the godless world of rock music, halter tops, and Halloween apples with razor blades inside them. Some have restaurants. Some have free gyms. Some have movie theaters. Some have brothels with hookers dressed like popular Old Testament characters. Well, maybe not that last thing, but megachurches try to provide alternatives to everything secular. And in sleepy suburbs megachurches are a more exciting place to hang out than the 7-Eleven parking lot. Though if you're underage and looking for a guy in a Camaro to buy you beer, 7-Eleven is still the place to go.

It's fun being surrounded by people who say "awesome" a lot: We don't know why evangelicals say "awesome" a lot. But they do. Maybe they think it's hip slang. Maybe it's the popularity of the Christian praise song "Our God is an Awesome God." Or maybe it's because being surrounded by people who say "awesome" makes you feel, well, *awesome*.

Megachurch Hall of Fame

10. Radiant Church, Surprise, Arizona: Operates a publicly funded school that doubles as a church recruiting center. Radiant spends $16,000 annually on Krispy Kreme donuts. Pastor Lee McFarland told the *New York Times*: "We want the church to look like a mall. We want you to come in here and say, 'Dude, where's the cinema?'"

9. Brentwood Baptist Church, Houston, Texas: Has its own McDonald's, complete with golden arches and a drive-through.

8. Southeast Christian, Louisville, Kentucky: Has a gym, sixteen basketball courts, a rock-climbing wall, and a member of its congregation invented the Greenlee Communion Dispensing Machine, which can fill forty Communion cups at once in a matter of seconds.

7. Willow Creek Community Church, South Barrington, Illinois: Their pastor, Bill Hybels, is often credited as being the daddy of the modern megachurch. He moonlights as a megachurch guru and has trained over ten thousand pastors on how to get fuge. (That's a sinner's contraction for *fucking huge*.)

6. Solid Rock Church, Monroe, Ohio: The home of the world's largest Jesus statue. Towering over their baptismal pool at sixty-two feet (six stories), it also has a forty-foot cross at its base. Called the "Kings of Kings" statue, it cost $250,000 to construct.

5. North Point Ministries, Alabama/Georgia/Michigan: One of many franchised McChurches in the country, sometimes known as satellite churches. North Point avoided investing in a larger building by beaming their senior pastor in high-definition video to nine daughter churches in several states. Grimace, the Fry Guys, and the Hamburglar hope to get jobs as praise-and-worship ministers in one of their nine affiliated locations. North Point Ministries is more high-tech than most companies; they have three hundred networked computers.

4. Crossover Community Church, Tampa, Florida: The hip-hop church. Reminiscent of a nightclub, Crossover is decorated with

---

 Quick fact: 63 percent of all African Americans claim to be born-again or evangelical. (Gallup Poll, 2005)

graffiti, has a pulpit designed to look like a large spray can, features break-dancing, hip-hop music, and is pastored by a rapper named Urban D who calls himself a "player" on his church Web site. The church covers topics like "what it means to be God's illest." Crossover is slightly too small to qualify as a megachurch, but makes the cut for sheer innovation.

3. The Potter's House, Dallas, Texas: T. D. Jakes's megachurch is the largest African-American megachurch in the nation. They have their own magazine, publishing house, daily talk show, a prison ministry that broadcasts to over 260 prisons, and their own recording studio that has produced a Grammy Award–winning gospel record.

2. Saddleback Church, Lake Forest, California: Bar codes are assigned to babies checked into the nursery to avoid losing them at the Purpose Driven pastor's (Rick Warren) enormous megachurch.

1. Lakewood Church, Houston, Texas: The largest megachurch in the country. Joel Osteen's church meets in the former home of the Houston Rockets and has already outgrown the arena.

The Megachurch of the Profit, Creflo Dollar

"It is easier for a camel to go through the eye of a needle than for a rich man to enter into the kingdom of God." (Matthew 19:24)

Megachurches are big business. Most have million-dollar budgets. And similar to big corporations like Capital One or Initech, most

I've heard Creflo Dollar speak, and I like what he says sometimes, but he always brings it all back to money. Like you can't be poor and a good Christian at the same time. That's not what God says. You don't need an airplane to be a good Christian.

megachurches are filled with people who own at least five pairs of pleated khakis. Not surprisingly, the big budgets are often accompanied by big criticism. Especially from secular elitists propagating the agenda of the Beast. Nevertheless, given the scrutiny that accompanied the televangelist scandals of the eighties—remember Jim Bakker's air-conditioned doghouse?—most million-dollar pastors go out of their way to avoid drawing attention to their fat wallets. Now that they've made their fortunes, pastors like Rick Warren and Joel Osteen have even stopped taking salaries. Today, the media, the IRS, and cynical churchgoers burned by the televangelists of the eighties have all joined God's lookout, searching for camels trying to sneak through the needle's eye.

Georgia's Rev. Creflo Dollar, on the other hand, has an altogether different approach. He owns two Rolls-Royces. He has a mansion in Georgia and a $2.5 million apartment in Manhattan. He travels with bodyguards. He has his own private jet. He wears custom-made, three-piece suits. Most conspicuously, he goes by the name *Dollar*, which, though he denies it, is rumored to not be his God-given moniker. Who would have guessed? Reverend Dollar speaks with the affected cadences of a Southern Cold War–era minister, but injects his sermons with the type of pop culture Ebonics you'd expect from an *In Living Color* repeat. The creators of *The Simpsons* couldn't concoct a more comical caricature. Unfortunately, Dollar is real.

God Help Us: Dollar Is One of the Most Influential Pastors in the Country

Like Joel Osteen, Rev. Dollar preaches the prosperity gospel and has his own megachurch: the World Changers Church in Atlanta. It's the second largest African-American church in the country. Unlike Joel Osteen, Creflo Dollar has no shame. He fully embraces the bling bling and tells his congregation outwardly that he wants their money. "If you sow a seed with your tithes and offerings today," he said in a recent sermon, "God is gonna bless you with a fruitful harvest."

And on Dollar's video *Laying Hold of Your Inheritance: Getting What's Rightfully Yours*, he shamelessly proclaims his mantra: "I want my stuff." In Dollar's world, driving a Rolls-Royce paid for by his congregation isn't decadent. It's a testament to his church that following God assures prosperity. Not to mention that he, well, gets to drive a Rolls-Royce.

The Prosperity Gospel Leaders

And their financial transparency grades (from MinistryWatch), based upon how forthcoming they are with their financial records.

Kenneth Copeland: F

Creflo Dollar: F

Joyce Meyer: C

T. D. Jakes: F

Paul Crouch/Trinity Broadcasting: C

Benny Hinn: F

Satan: score N/A

    formerly, Jim Bakker

    and Robert Tilton

A Sermon in the Life of Creflo Dollar: Buckets of God's Love

Every Saturday, Reverend Dollar flies in his private jet to New York from his home in Atlanta for an evening service, generally held at the theater in Madison Square Garden. He addresses thousands of enthusiastic, mainly African-American evangelicals and, of course, collects an offering. The service is apparently where he gets his petty cash for gold cufflinks and dinners at Red Lobster, since his twenty-five-thousand-member Georgia church already has an estimated $80 million budget, according to the *New York Times*.

At a recent service, a woman dressed in a corporate-looking power suit spoke in tongues into a microphone while an exhilarated audience chanted along in expectation of Reverend Dollar's arrival. We began to worry the crowd might grab some pitchforks, light some torches, and march us out of the church chanting. We were, after all, sinning foreigners who didn't speak their indecipherable language.

When Dollar arrived onstage wearing his signature pin-striped suit and bouncing enthusiastically like a man possessed, he jubilantly proclaimed, "If you've been living from paycheck to paycheck, get your faith jacked up. God's getting ready to deliver you." The crowd went wild. We sealed an offering envelope with some quarters inside, worried that failing to do so could cause a riot.

"God tells you," Dollar continued, looking like he might burst a blood vessel in his temple, "to do more than what you can afford to do."

As the collection buckets—yes, Reverend Dollar uses buckets—began to be passed around, Dollar shouted: "It's opportunity for prosperity time!" His congregation took to their feet, excitedly waving cash-filled envelopes above their heads, as if they'd all been selected to play *The Price Is Right.* After all, Dollar had informed the crowd that they were *guaranteed* a large "harvest" if they planted an ample "seed." We sincerely hoped it worked out for them. Most of the churchgoers we'd spoken to before the service were from New York neighborhoods more blessed by graffiti and left-behind schools than by God's prosperity. Maybe the *harvest* of which Dollar spoke was City Harvest, a local nonprofit that feeds the hungry.

"Give money and money shall be given unto you," Dollar continued. "*This* is how you make a living. *That job* is not how you make your living."

Soon after, Dollar thanked God for George Bush and went on a tirade about the growing abomination of gays in Greenwich Village. When he began muttering something about earthquakes, tsunamis, and bird flu epidemics being a sign of the last days, we knew we had to leave. We couldn't breathe. We'd like to claim our breathlessness was the result of being submerged beneath stacks of cash pouring from Heaven. A harvest being reaped from the spare change we'd sewn. But that's not what happened. We'd simply been punched in the gut by the Church of the Almighty Profit, Creflo Dollar.

 Quick fact: All Saints Episcopal Church's tax-exempt status was placed under investigation by the IRS because of an antiwar sermon by their pastor. James Dobson's status remains unquestioned, even though he supported the preemptive invasion of Iraq as "necessary and just" and directly endorsed conservative Republican Pat Toomey in a 2004 primary.
(*LA Times*, 2005, and *Harvard Political Review*, 2005)

HOLY SH!T

Abstinence-Only Programs and Silver Ring Thing

The federal government spends an estimated $170 million in tax dollars on abstinence-only programs annually. Federally funded groups like True Love Waits, Silver Ring Thing, and Sex Respect are alternatives to traditional "graphic" sex education classes and teach horny teens to wait until marriage to have sex. Silver Ring Thing, for instance, encourages kids to make an abstinence-only pledge "before almighty God" before they are given a ring inscribed with a phrase that reads, "God wants you to be holy, so you should keep clear of sexual sin." The program was founded by an evangelical minister and has received over a million in tax dollars.

By federal law, abstinence programs like Silver Ring Thing cannot promote condoms, *they can only discuss condoms' failure rates and their ineffectiveness in the prevention of disease and pregnancy*. Programs that promote condom use risk losing their funding. A study published in the *Journal of Adolescent Health* found that teens who go through abstinence-only programs are much more likely to have anal and oral sex than non-pledgers, often without protection, since they've been taught that condoms fail. There are over a hundred abstinence-only programs in the country and one-third of the schools in the country have adopted the programs. The programs received an estimated $900 million in federal funds from 2000 to 2006.[3]

---

[3]Following a suit from the ACLU, Silver Ring Thing lost its eligibility for federal funding in 2006 for evangelizing on Uncle Sam's dime. Given the multitude of like-minded abstinence programs (many of which overtly try to convince children to commit their lives to Christ), the victory was a small one. The White House brags that 102 abstinence programs have been federally funded since 2001 and plans to continue spending close to $200 million a year on programs similar to Silver Ring Thing. One down, 101 to go.

Partial List of Moronic Claims Found in Federally Funded Abstinence-Only Programs (According to a Congressional Report by Rep. Henry A. Waxman)

- Half of all gay teens have HIV.
- Touching a person's genitals can cause pregnancy.
- A fetus will become a "thinking person" at forty-three days.
- Men find happiness in "accomplishments."
- Women find happiness in their "relationships."
- HIV can be contracted through sweat and/or tears.
- Sex can cause mental health problems.
- Premature births are more likely after having an abortion.
- In regard to heterosexual sex, condoms have a 31 percent failure rate in the protection against HIV.
- Women "are more prone to suicide" after an abortion.
- 14 percent of women who "use condoms scrupulously for birth control" will get pregnant within a year's time.
- Legal, elective abortions cause sterility approximately 10 percent of the time.
- Fetuses have "Twenty-four chromosomes from the mother and twenty-four chromosomes from the father."

 Quick fact: Many evangelical and conservative groups have voiced opposition to a new vaccine that prevents the spread of genital warts, a virus that is a leading cause of cervical cancer. They feel that vaccinating kids against the virus removes a useful deterrent to premarital sex. Similar arguments have been made by conservatives who are opposed to testing teens for HIV. (*The New Yorker*, 2006)

Teens who take the pledge are more likely to have anal
and oral sex than non-pledgers.

Rick Warren, the Evangelical Jimmy Buffet

3

Rick Warren and the Seeker-Sensitive Pastorpreneurs

Rick Warren: The Evangelical Jimmy Buffet

Fire and Brimstone Score: 5

Nutshell: Hawaiian shirt–wearing evangelist and poster child of the most important development in the contemporary church, the seeker-sensitive movement.

Denomination: Southern Baptist

Born: 1954, a fifth-generation minister

Defining Quote: "I've got a target. It's called the globe."

Quick Facts about Rick Warren

- Wrote *The Purpose Driven Life*, the bestselling hardcover nonfiction book in history.
- Pastor of twenty-two thousand at Saddleback megachurch in Lake Forest, California.
- Rwanda's president recently declared the country the first "Purpose Driven Nation."
- Warren's 40 Days of Purpose seminars, based on his book, have been taught in 10 percent of the nation's churches.
- A quote from the pastor was recently printed on a Starbucks cup.
- Warren's follow-up to *The Purpose Driven Life, Getting Dressed Up for Church Harshes Jesus' Mellow, Dude,* is due out some time before the Antichrist comes to power.

The Purpose Driven Pastor

No wonder sinners, liberals, and Volvo owners are so out of the loop. Rick Warren is one of the most influential leaders in the country, yet most people outside of the church know next to nothing about him. The megachurch pastor and author of the Christian devotional book *The Purpose Driven Life*, Rick Warren has been called the probable successor to Billy Graham as our nation's pastor. He's ministered to leaders such as George Bush, Bill Clinton, and Rupert Murdoch, and claims to have personally signed a copy of *The Purpose Driven Life* at the request of Fidel Castro, though some of the aforementioned, obviously, are still going to hell.

Rick Warren's influence is perplexing. After all, he *really* believes that David killed a giant with a slingshot and other biblical stories you're apt to see reinterpreted on *Xena: Warrior Princess*. He also believes that Noah had never seen rain before the Flood, because in Old Testament times "God irrigated the earth from the ground up." Even more terrifying, Warren apparently thinks people don't mind looking at his man-feet, since the laid-back pastor has preached sermons wearing sandals. Yet he has influenced millions.

Warren's *The Purpose Driven Life* encourages people to discover their own God-given purpose, through forty daily readings, to achieve happiness in life. Warren's God's-your-buddy preaching style—and his Hawaiian shirt collection—define *his* God-given purpose. Warren is the Jimmy Buffet of evangelical culture.

QUICK QUIZ: Rick Warren has compared homosexuality to having sex with which of the following animals:

A. A cheetah
B. A cocker spaniel
C. A horse
D. An iguana
E. One of them pretty long-haired Lhasa apsos that always wears bows on their heads

[Correct answer: C]

If I start having anal sex with my [male] roommate, should we qualify for *special* benefits? I have legitimate feelings for my buddy's boxer dog. I think he's great. Should we qualify for a civil union? . . . Why not have a civil union with members of your family and have a big orgy every night? Where do you draw the line?

Building a Church in Margaritaville

When Warren founded Saddleback Church in 1980, he didn't select Orange County's Saddleback Valley hoping to meet Seth Cohen from the *The O.C.* But the sinners from that hit TV show were definitely the immoral types he was looking to recruit. Warren wanted to lead a church for the "unchurched" and studied population demographics to see which areas in the United States had the largest unsaved communities before deciding on Saddleback County. After all, who wants to go to a church filled with a bunch of grown adults who think *The Lion, the Witch and the Wardrobe* is literature's pinnacle achievement? Then, Warren prayed about his decision. He prayed the shit out of that decision.

Today, Saddleback is commonly referred to as being "seeker-sensitive," a casual church with all the fixin's where sinners—who Warren endearingly refers to as "unrepentant pagans"—will feel at home. Seeker-sensitive churches are strictly orchestrated to appeal to sinners. Church slogans at Saddleback Church promise "God's Extreme Makeover," and sermons can be watched in a variety of settings, including an on-premises café equipped with live feeds of the service. Seeker-sensitive churches, like Rick Warren's and Joel Osteen's, are in the business of marketing themselves to sinners.

 Quick fact: Five out of ten evangelicals have no college education. (Gallup Poll, 2005)

Quick Facts about Warren's Saddleback Church

- Collected $7 million in cash on one Sunday.
- Bar codes are assigned to babies checked in to the nursery to avoid losing them.
- Has an estimated three thousand church-based small groups.
- Provides several service styles, including gospel, guitar-driven, and even "hula and island-style."
- Has a 120-acre campus, three hundred employees, and over sixty daughter churches.

Is Rick Warren Political?

Rick Warren routinely claims to not be a part of the evangelical right when speaking to secular elitists at the *New York Times* and elsewhere, but he's playing both sides of the fence. Warren has gone on record claming that he's "firmly a cultural conservative." He also believes opposing abortion, gay rights, stem cell research, human cloning, and euthanasia are "non-negotiable" and "not even debatable" for people of values. He called the Terry Schiavo debacle "an atrocity worthy of Nazism."

Prior to the 2004 election, Warren set up voter registration booths on Saddleback's church patio. Most tellingly, he sent letters to 150,000 pastors insisting they encourage their congregations to vote for Bush. So when Warren claims he's not a part of the evangelical right, it's most likely because he's pissed at Pat Robertson for making him sit in a cubicle next to Benny Hinn and the fax machine in the evangelical right's crummy branch office in California.

I think that abstinence should be taught, but I also think that education about condoms should be taught. . . . You can't just ignore that STDs are out there. Some kids are gonna have sex.

The Purpose Driven Censor

First Amendment speech is apparently "non-negotiable" in Warren's world too. He tried to strong-arm the first-time author of *Pyro-Marketing* into removing all mentions of *The Purpose Driven Life* from his book, since Warren didn't like the way the book candidly addressed the aggressive marketing campaign of *PDL*. *PyroMarketing* author Greg Stielstra (who helped market *PDL*) was outraged that a better-selling author was "allowed to interfere with the content of [his] book." Stielstra says he ultimately reached a compromise with the publisher, HarperCollins/Zondervan, but the book's publication was delayed for several months due to Warren's attempts to censor its content. The final version was slightly altered to appease Warren.

Stielstra says he was surprised by the publisher's requests and deeply disappointed by Warren's actions: "I've offered to fly to California or meet him in other cities along his travels so we can resolve our differences according to Jesus's instructions in Matthew 18, but Warren has never replied."

Onward Christian Parrotheads: The "Global Decade"

As Warren's fame, influence, and appetite for jalapeño poppers continues to grow, he's shifted his focus to ending global social problems. Warren's trademark outreach program is called the PEACE Plan, an ambitious project to link up a network of "10 million churches" across the globe to end poverty, battle AIDS, and, of course, deliver

Stryper. Switchfoot. Sufjan Stevens. Scott Stapp . . . all the "s" sounds associated with Christian Rock . . . reminds me of the sssoundsss of the ssserpent hissself. It could not be more clear to my molten eye: Christian Rock is the devil's music!

Hawaiian shirts to the unconverted. The pastor even recently joined forces with social activist/rocker Bono at Live 8, Warren's saintlike powers of forgiveness permitting him to overlook one of humanity's greatest transgressions: *Achtung Baby.*

In 2005, Rick Warren addressed the United Nations and the Council on Foreign Relations to discuss his global social plans. Even though the food scraps dangling from John Bolton's mustache recently brought sustenance to a plague-stricken village in Uganda, Warren claims that the UN and secular relief groups can't solve the world's big problems, such as hunger and Third World poverty. It's up to the churches and secular relief groups says Warren, perhaps stating a self-fulfilling prophecy given the increased diversion of federal funds from the established relief groups in favor of faith-based initiatives.

Outside of this country, Warren's PEACE Plan is gaining momentum. In 2005, Rwanda's president, Paul Kagame, declared the country the first "Purpose Driven Nation," hugging the pastor for the cameras in expectation of Warren's aid. Hallelujah! Soon Rwandans, newly converted by soccer moms in Gap khakis, will be able to become purpose driven as they set up small groups *in their own churches.* The "I Can't Read the White Man's Leather Book Because I'm Illiterate" and the "Sucking on Sugarcane for Sustenance" small groups are both bound to be popular.

The Purpose Hidden Agenda

> *"Jesus said, 'This Gospel shall be preached into all the world to every nation and then the end shall come.' He's not coming back until that happens. . . . The question is will we get to be the ones who get to be in on it or not. Will we be the generation who says, 'Let's make this happen!' "*

—Warren, discussing the launch of the PEACE Plan

 Quick fact: Eagle Brook Church in Minnesota installed cineplex-style cup holders into the seats so that worshippers could raise their hands during the service without fear of spilling their lattes. *(St. Paul Pioneer Press, 2006)*

Good intentions notwithstanding, Warren's global evangelical out-reach has a dark side; namely, he's in the process of fulfilling what he believes to be biblical prophecy. Like most evangelicals, Warren bases his ministry on Matthew 24:14, the Great Commission: the belief that Jesus will return to Earth after the globe has been evangelized. Not co-incidentally, when introducing his PEACE Plan, he claimed he wanted to see an "evangelization of the planet." And addressing Saddleback about global AIDS initiatives, Rick's wife, Kay, called the battle against AIDS a spiritual battle that could "speed up the return of our King of kings." Warren's purpose hidden agenda is the hastening of the Second Coming of Jesus. "He's not coming back," Warren says, "until that happens." He's not coming back until you put some shoes on, either, Rick.

Warren in Context

On his ministry: "The Purpose Driven paradigm is the Intel chip for the twenty-first-century church and the Windows system of the twenty-first-century church."

On natural disasters: "The Bible teaches that since sin entered the world, way back with the very first human beings, we have lived in an imperfect, broken planet, and that causes hurricanes and tornadoes."

The Seeker-Sensitive Pastorpreneurs

Attracting the Sinners: The Seeker-Sensitive Movement

Most of the churches that have made it to the top of the food chain today, like Saddleback and Lakewood, have done so by being what evangelicals call seeker-sensitive—that is, churches that pay attention to the wants and needs of "unchurched" sinners turned off by orga-nized religion and crazy-eyed preachers with aerosol pompadours. Seeker-sensitive churches try to get sinners to attend by using the-atrics, gimmicks, feel-good preaching, and in Carson Valley Christian Center's case, Christian martial arts classes where you can learn to kick butt "the Christian warrior way." On the surface, seeker-sensitive churches usually seem tolerant and progressive, but as we'll demon-strate, they're pulling a bait and switch.

Many churches have become multimillion-dollar companies that, like any other business, want to keep growing. It's logical that they would want to attract the unchurched. Sinners represent the largest untapped potential tithing demographic. And if a seeker-sensitive pastor is able to attract a "pagan" in "shorts and a Budweiser T-shirt" (Rick Warren's words), the last thing he wants to do is offend him. He could lose his business to the Church of the Redeemer down the street. Knowing this, pastors like Warren and Osteen have let the coals cool down a bit on their fire and brimstone to keep the crowds from turning away. The Jesus of the seeker-sensitive movement doesn't walk on water. He walks on eggshells.

I've been known to knock back a Crown and 7 or a few margaritas. There's nothing wrong with getting a little lit [on alcohol] as long as I don't look at women or get too cross-eyed to drive.

Seeker-Sensitive Sinner Bait

Revival Ministries International, Tampa Bay, Florida: Gave away a Hummer as an outreach tool to draw in "unchurched" seekers.

Christ's Church of the Valley, Peoria, Arizona: Offered a U2 ticket giveaway to attract sinners.

LifePointe Christian Church, Charlotte, North Carolina: Generated church brand awareness among non-churchgoers by giving away thousands of Frisbees and water bottles emblazoned with their church logo.

New Life Christian Church, Centreville, Virginia: Has an ice cream truck that drives around town giving out free ice cream to attract new members.

Clearview Community Church, Sioux City, Iowa: Offered free gas to first-time visitors in response to high gas prices. "We are so confident that our worship service will be the best hour of your week," said Clearview's pastor, "that we are willing to pay for your gas to get here and back."

Bill Hybels and Seeker-Sensitive Sinner Psychology

Though Warren and Osteen have become the patron saints of the seeker-sensitive movement, they owe much to pastor Bill Hybels. Before Rick had ironed his first palm-tree-print baptismal robe, Hybels was busy creating what has become known as the first seeker-sensitive megachurch, Willow Creek in South Barrington, Illinois. In the mid-seventies, Hybels polled his community and used market research to see what unchurched people liked and disliked about church and then re-moved the obstacles. Today, his church has no steeple, no hymnals, no stained glass, and no intimidating religious crosses or symbols. Willow Creek's services are more like finely choreographed theater, climaxing with syrupy feel-good sermons designed to not offend. Hybels even lets newcomers remain anonymous, forgoing the potentially nerve-racking visitor's greeting and handshakes. The added benefit of the latter of course being that believers can avoid touching the plague-infected hands of sodomites and gays who stumble into the sanctuary. But even though it's a church for the unchurched, Hybels' twenty-thousand-member church is still overrun with Republicans and people who think Karl Rove is a cool guy, a deterrent of the highest degree for many sinners.

The Seeker-Sensitive Playa Hatas

Not surprisingly, the seeker-sensitive movement has its fair share of Christian critics, generally old-school Southern Baptists from Alabama who think the movement panders to sinners, waters down the gospel, and promotes the heresy that proper ladies can wear jeans to church. These critics also tend to enjoy a good joke about how "Orientals" eat poodles.

 Quick fact: Republicans are far more likely to say they are born-again (52 percent) than Democrats (36 percent) or independents (32 percent).   (Gallup Poll, 2005)

Other critics include evangelical Gen Xers who've become frustrated with churches that shamelessly market themselves to the public with ads and gimmicks, as many seeker-sensitive churches notoriously do (see Emerging Church, p. 186). All the same, the seeker-sensitive movement is arguably the most notable trend in the contemporary church.

I think everyone will be brought into the presence of God when they die and be given a second chance. Parents love their children enough to forgive them and God's love is greater than man's. I don't believe in hell as a *final* destination.

Unsuccessful Church Slogans

Most seeker-sensitive churches have easy-to-digest slogans and mission statements to make things simple for the unchurched. For instance, the Without Walls International Church's slogan is "The Perfect Church for People Who Aren't." Here are some sample slogans that aren't quite as strong:

"Gays Welcome, Just Stay Away from the Nursery"
"Preaching the Whole Gospel, Even the Creepy Stuff"
"Home of the Wet T-shirt Baptism"
"Now with Xboxes and Movie Theater Popcorn"
"Taking Your Money, Spreading His Word"
"Now Guaranteed to Be 78 Percent Less Judgmental"
"Home of the 33⅓ Percent Tithe"

The Pastorpreneurs

Megachurch pastors today don't just need a master's in theology, they need marketing degrees. From offering free wi-fi and purchasing television ads to selecting the right seat cushions, attracting churchgoers today has become a precise science. Thankfully, pastorpreneurs like Warren and Hybels have doctorates in megachurch building, and have begun teaching up-and-coming pastors the tricks of the trade.

They share their knowledge in books and at conferences, for a fee, and provide tools to help churches grow. Now up-and-coming pastors can learn how to grow their own megachurches. And along the way, they can observe how masters like Warren endorse Republican candidates from the altar in code language, without losing their tax-exempt status. Here are Rick Warren's and Bill Hybels's church-growth ministries.

Rick Warren's Purpose Driven Ministries: Warren's trained over 400,000 pastors, often charging up to $150 a head to attend church-growth conferences. His church-growth company, Purpose Driven Ministries, has a $39 million budget and provides interactive preaching resources to 150,000 pastors. Wal-Mart, Ford, Coca-Cola, the United States Air Force, the United States Postal Service, and the NBA have even participated in Warren's "40 Days of Purpose" campaigns. He's made so much money, in fact, he's become a "reverse tither," giving away 90 percent of his income to the church and another 5 percent, apparently, to the Windjammer Catch-a-Wave Discount Shirt Shack.

Bill Hybels and the Willow Creek Association (WCA): Hybels founded the Willow Creek Association in 1991 to teach pastors how to make their churches bigger. WCA now trains over 100,000 pastors and leaders annually. The focus of a recent Harvard Business School case study, the Willow Creek Association ranks in the top 5 percent of the major brands in the country, according to *Business Week*. WCA member churches pay $249 a year to join and are given access to WCA-approved "service builders," such as sermons and theater scripts. WCA is likely considering free Hawaiian shirts and electric goatee trimmers for aspiring pastors as well.

The Purpose Driven Handbook for Winning Over Sinners: So what do pastorpreneurs like Warren and Hybels teach aspiring

---

 Quick fact: Motive Marketing, a Christian marketing company, was hired by Disney to promote *The Lion, the Witch and the Wardrobe* to evangelicals. Motive Marketing distinguished itself from other Christian marketers in its promotion of *The Passion*, which grossed over $600 million.

(*Washington Post*, 2005)

megachurch pastors anyway? Warren's seeker-sensitive church-growth handbook, *The Purpose Driven Church*, is a revealing window into some of the soul-winning tactics they promote at their conferences.

Warren says the first thing you need to discern as a pastor is your desired demographic. He refers to his target as "Saddleback Sam," and in-

Doesn't attend church because "it's boring." Secretly worries his stomach may growl during the sermons.

Thinks about the afterlife sometimes, especially during commercial breaks of *Buffy the Vampire Slayer*.

Fears his ethereal gaze is mistaken for a vacant stare.

Wants more from life than the apartment in his aunt's basement.

Cares about values and watches FOX News because they use the shiniest colors.

Likes contemporary music

Prefers writing with pencils to writing with pens.

Knows high school rings never go out of style.

Would prefer a Vienna sausage and Kool-Aid communion to Welch's and Wafers.

Is comfortable with technology and has a Chewbacca screen saver.

Feels more at home in a casual church where he can wear his drawstring khakis and the shoes he bought at the Comfort Zone.

Richmond Ronnie

Rick Warren encourages pastors to identify their "unchurched" demographic using profiles like "Saddleback Sam" and "Dallas Doug." Here's Richmond Ronnie.

cludes a photo of a cell-phone-toting man in pleated slacks who is "young," "white-collar," "smug," and "health and fitness are high priorities for him." Judging from the businessman-in-Sally-Jessy-Rafael-glasses image Warren chose to illustrate his target, Saddleback Sam is also that yuppie asshole who interrogated us in a job interview about the meaning of the word "synergy." Warren says he has a hobby of collecting "evangelistic profiles" like "Dallas Doug," "Memphis Mike," and "Atlanta Al." Here's one of our own (previous page), inspired by Warren, "Richmond Ronnie."

QUICK QUIZ (PRAY ON THE WEAK): In *The Purpose Driven Church*, Rick Warren outlines the ten types of sinners who are the most receptive to receiving Christ. Circle the *two* that *do not* appear on his *list*.

A. Alcohol/drug addicts
B. The terminally ill
C. Individuals undergoing a divorce
D. The really really smart
E. The poor/recently unemployed
F. People with toupees

[Correct answers: D, F]

Them Smelly Sinners: Advice from Rick Warren

"If your church is serious about reaching the unchurched," Warren writes in *The Purpose Driven Church*, "you must be willing to put up with people who have a lot of problems. Fishing is often smelly and messy." Evidently Warren prefers the English Leather and hamburger smell of evangelicals, but nonetheless has written extensively on how to attract smelly sinners. Given the success of Warren's and Hybels's books and growth conferences, it's not surprising how many churches conform to their suggestions. Here are some tips from *The Purpose Driven Church* to help make churches bigger and filled with the stinky smell of sinners:

1. Get a shirt with parrots on it: "I intentionally dress down," writes Warren, "to match the mind-set of those I'm trying to reach."

2. Be insincere: "I became like a Southern Californian, in order to win Southern Californians."

3. Use polls and surveys to determine what your community needs: "I know of one church that discovered through a survey that the number-one felt need in their community was potty training. . . ."

4. Get comfy seats: "Uncomfortable seating is a distraction the devil loves to use."

5. Avoid scary religious symbols: ". . . the unchurched are confused by chalices, crowns, and doves with fire coming out their tails."

6. Orchestrate the music to manipulate the weak: Play upbeat happy music to "loosen up the tense muscles," followed by "joyful" and "meditative" songs before moving to a "commitment song," such as "I Want to Be More Like You," that utilizes the "first person singular."

7. Avoid discussing denominations since they can be divisive: "Clear up the misconceptions *after* they [have] accepted Christ."

8. Keep it *real* simple: Create sermon titles that "sound like *Reader's Digest* articles," Warren suggests.

9. A useful joke to use if someone complains about organized religion: "Then you will like [our church]. We're disorganized religion!"

10. Hurray for Freaky Friday and Weird Wednesday! "Design one worship service to edify believers and another to evangelize the unchurched . . . our believers' service is on Wednesday."

11. If the above doesn't achieve conversions, just make the lights hot enough to fry them godless sinners: "Brighten up your environment . . . replace all the lightbulbs in your worship center with twice the watts."

The Seeker-Sensitive Call to Civic Responsibility

The evangelical right has come under attack in recent years for having tunnel vision on pro-family issues, at the expense of more "liberal" social issues like poverty and the environment. More progressive evangelicals, such as Jim Wallis and the members of the National Council of Churches, have emphasized that the evangelical right places too much emphasis on abortion and the evils of *Will & Grace*. Still, the evangelical right's preoccupation with abortion and homosexuality, at the expense of larger social concerns, has become what many have called a "marketing problem" for seeker-sensitive evangelicals looking to recruit sinners.

As Bill Hybels told *Business Week*: "[We] have a lot of seekers who will come to Willow and ask, 'What are you doing about AIDS? How are you responding to the tsunami? How do you care for the poor?' And our answer to those questions weighs into their decision-making process."

As Hybels suggests, why would liberals, who typically have higher moral authority on issues such as welfare and the environment, want to join a distracted church that's neurotically obsessed with outing gay cartoon characters?

With the smell of backlash in the air, the National Association of Evangelicals (p. 168) released a high-profile document in late 2004 calling for increased civic engagement. "An Evangelical Call to Civic Responsibility" addressed the need to inject a little Jesus into issues like AIDS, poverty, and the environment. Disappointingly, in the months following the NAE's pronouncement, the largest debate in churches had little to do with increased civic engagement. It was whether to label the jeans rack at JCPenney with a sign that read "holiday" or "Christmas" sale.

Ron Sider, the author of *Scandal of the Evangelical Conscience*, was involved in drafting the "Call to Civic Responsibility." Sider recalls Focus on the Family's Vice President of Public Policy, Tom Minnery, walking into an early meeting about the document and saying, "Let's

It's our job [as evangelicals] to tell gays that what they're doing is not okay with God. I've got friends who have church leaders who tell them that lifestyle is okay, which makes me mad, because leaders should preach the truth. I can't get with that.

not make this about global warming." Evidently, dudes who make out with each other are a larger threat to evangelical households than, say, the billions of tons of seawater threatening to submerge their homes when the polar icecaps begin to melt. Sider says there's "no doubt" that many of the leaders involved in drafting the "Call to Civic Responsibility" definitely want to "keep the focus on abortion and family issues."

The religious author and Wheaton College professor Mark Noll argues that the church has always been civically engaged on a wide array of issues like poverty. Still, the full extent of the NAE's sincerity is questionable, especially on the issue of the environment, which incidentally evangelicals refer to as "creation care." The NAE's vice president, Richard Cizik, for instance, has rejected offers to cooperate with the Sierra Club and the National Wildlife Federation, since they are secular. And when asked what his plan would be to help the environment, the NAE's president, Ted Haggard (p. 115) seems to think Wal-Mart is going to stop global warming:

> The environmentalists have failed because they're Socialists. . . . Put the guys who are distributing Coke all over the world, and causing Wal-Mart to grow all over the world, put *those* guys in a room and you'll come up with some real solutions for the environment. . . . A pro-business system creates a cleaner environment.

Even more telling, Haggard's New Life Church has fifteen hundred small groups, covering every interest niche from volleyball to debunking evolution to praise aerobics. Nevertheless, there are zero environmental groups at New Life, unless you count their "Entrepreneurs Like Us" small group, since apparently pro-business, pro–free market capitalists are God's secret weapon to cleaning up the air.

 Quick fact: "You can get the [HIV] virus in tears and sweat."
(Evangelical senator, and doctor, Bill Frist on ABC News's *This Week*)

In 2006, a coalition of evangelicals (including Rick Warren) launched their follow-up to the 2004 "Call to Civic Responsibility," called the "Evangelical Climate Initiative." The initiative was an attempt to curb climate change with television and radio spots and by promoting "cost-effective, market-based" pro-business solutions. Richard Cizik, Ted Haggard, and the NAE—not to mention Chuck Colson, James Dobson, D. James Kennedy, Donald Wildmon, Richard Land, and a majority of the evangelical community—refused to back the initiative, claiming there is no consensus on the science of global warming.

Apparently, some science-wary evangelicals need to go back and take another one of Warren's or Hybels's seeker-sensitive classes. Their empty pronouncements haven't fooled us wayward sinners.

HOLY SH!T

Youth Groups Submitted by Pastors on youthpastor.com with Names Derived from "Generation X"

X + Alt *X stands for Christ and alt stands for alternative.*

X UnderGround *Christ first in the basement we meet in!*

X Factor *Our purpose: Exalt, Expand, Extend.*

X Ministries *Xamine, Xtra Mile & Xtreme*

X Squared *Xtreme Xaltation*

X ZONE *Connecting today's youth*

X-4-J *X-Treme-4-JESUS*

X-ample *Be an example to the believers.*

X-cellent Generation *A generation that will turn the world upside down with the gospel*

X-cite *Getting Generation X excited for Jesus*

X-claim! *Proclaiming our faith in Jesus Christ and claiming this generation for the Lord*

X-PLOSION *Youth exploding onto the Christ scene*

X-preszo *We do this with a purpose*

X-S.T.R.E.A.M. *X-Sinners Totally Radical Empowering All Mankind*

X-Scape *Turning the hearts of youth & families to God and each other*

X-Sight *Extreme Youth Getting Vision*

X.X.X. *X-cited, X-travagant, X-generation!*

X4J *eXtreme for Jesus*

Xccelerate *Spreading the Gospel . . . FAST*

XChanged *X-changing Darkness for Light*

XEROKS *To duplicate Disciples*

XFACTOR *Don't Forget to Factor Generation X*

Xplode Youth *Dynamic Teens Fired Up*

Xposure *Exists to train students to "expose" their light of Jesus Christ into a dark world.*
Xpress *Xpress yourself in Christ*
XRDS *Teens at CrossRoads of life*
XTC *Xtreme teens for CHRIST*
XtraOrdinary *Youth Not ordinary*
Xtreme Vision *Armed and Dangerous*
Xtreme180 *A Complete Turnaround for God*
Xtremeoutcry *We will not let the rocks cry out in our place*
XYZ *Xtreme Young Zealous for Christ*

 Quick fact: Thomas Jefferson compiled his own version of the Bible, stripping it of its "artificial vestments." The Jefferson Bible contains no miracles and Jesus's virgin birth and resurrection have been removed. *(Harper's, 2005)*

Forget the gays . . . God hates shrimp!

4

The American Evangelicals: Christian by Birth, Republican by the Grace of God

> *"The real theological problem in America today is no longer the religious Right, but the nationalistic religion of the Bush administration."*
>
> Reverend Jim Wallis, from *God's Politics*

Until the sixties, evangelicals were just as likely to be Democrats as they were to be Republicans. Many evangelicals were on the front lines in the fight for women's suffrage, were vocal antiwar opponents, and led the fight for civil rights. Meanwhile, tent revival pastors fueled McCarthyism and covertly organized KKK meetings among their church elders. But the advent of the ERA Movement, the *Roe v. Wade* decision, and a godless culture filled with bra burnings and rock music created a unifying shift to the right. By the time abortion was made legal, many evangelicals found themselves curled up in the fetal position inside the headquarters of the RNC waiting for the world to end.

Following the election of Jimmy Carter, an outspoken Christian who was candid about being born-again, *Time* deemed 1976 "The Year of the Evangelical." Ironically, most evangelicals felt little kinship with this moderate Democratic president, given his support of ERA and his refusal to deny women the right to choose. Evangelical leaders like Jerry Falwell and Tim LaHaye believed the time had come to get evangelicals mobilized behind a candidate that represented *their* values. That candidate was Reagan, the first president to come to power with the help of what has come to be known as the Religious Right. Reagan was also the first high-level politician to work opposite a chimpanzee (as he did in *Bedtime for Bonzo*), a noble tradition carried on today by Vice President Dick Cheney.

The Trinity of American Christianity

The evangelical right has been busy organizing for over thirty years around the true trinity of American Christianity: the opposition to gay rights, abortion, and taxes. While lefties were busy shopping for organic lettuce, the evangelical right got savvy, nominating the types of tax-cutting, pro-family bobbleheads you'd want to take to Sizzler for a beer. But since many evangelicals are opposed to alcohol and their current bobblehead is a recovering alcoholic, they're stuck with O'Doul's. Clearly the Left has been sipping the hard stuff. They've become an unorganized group of tree-hugging wimps promoting a vaguely related assortment of social causes. They elect the types of bobbleheads you'd want to take to Sizzler for a Molotov cocktail.

Professor Mark Noll claims that evangelicals are an "American brand of Protestant Christianity." He's right. Their stubborn, tax-hating, rugged individualism is more a product of being American than it is of being Christian. After all, Jesus didn't give too many sermons on trickle-down economics or the inherent sinfulness of driving a foreign car.

In this chapter, we'll introduce you to some of the evangelical right's leaders, explain how *Christian* became synonymous with *Repub-*

I'm way Right. . . . I vote based on moral values and think the rest of the stuff, like the economy, will take care of itself. . . . I wouldn't vote for someone who was in favor of abortion or gay marriage. . . . As per the Iraq war, I'm not saying I fully support it, but it's up to God to judge Bush on that, not me.

lican, and equip you tax-'n'-spend sinners with the tools you need to debunk their often contradictory Bible-believin' ways.

Fundamental Contradictions: Picking and Choosing

Anyone who's read the Bible knows some of its disturbing content could give Grand Theft Auto a run for its money. War, murder, rape, slavery, men who wear sandals—parts of the Bible should come with adult content warning labels. If you want a peaceful religion, even Ted Haggard of the National Association of Evangelicals says, "choose Buddhism." Nevertheless, many evangelicals love the Bible so much they're willing to accept the whole darn thing, even the bizarre parts, at face value. They brag that they don't "pick and choose" from the Bible and refer to themselves as "Bible-believin'" Christians.

In Haiti there's a lot of voodoo. . . . I've heard of people being injected with poison from some rare fish that makes them seem dead. Then they're buried and dug up again later and they become like Zombies . . . once it's safer [in Haiti] I want to be a missionary there, a lot of those people need God.

Yet the glaring list of passages that typical evangelicals ignore could fill Falwell's dessert refrigerator at the Moral Majority to capacity. Leviticus 19:27, for instance, prohibits shaving, a commandment to which millions pay no attention. Likewise, Leviticus 19:19 forbids the wearing of mixed fibers. Needless to say, Pat Robertson is clearly guilty

 Quick fact: 64 percent of adults in the United States believe in Creationism. (Harris Poll, 2005)

of defying this commandment, given his collection of polyester flag ties. And most glaringly, as progressive evangelical leaders like Jim Wallis continue to drive home, there are roughly three thousand verses in the Bible devoted to helping the poor, yet typical evangelicals spend more time griping about the costs of welfare or bashing *The Da Vinci Code* than choosing to help the less fortunate. Truth be told, Bible-believin' evangelicals are more guilty of "picking and choosing" than the liberal Christians they often accuse of the same transgression. Here are some key verses Bible-believin' evangelicals *pick and choose* to ignore.

Key Verses Bible-Believin' Evangelicals *Pick and Choose* to Ignore

On slavery: "Slaves, submit yourselves to your masters with all respect, not only to those who are good and considerate, but also to those who are harsh." (1 Peter 2:18, NIV)

On rape: "If a man happens to meet a virgin who is not pledged to be married and rapes her and they are discovered, he shall pay the girl's father fifty shekels of silver." (Deuteronomy 22:28, NIV)

On women wearing veils: "And every woman who prays or prophesies with her head uncovered dishonors her head." (Corinthians 11:5, NIV)

On illegitimate children being barred from church: "A bastard shall not enter into the congregation of the Lord; even to his tenth generation shall he not enter into the congregation of the Lord." (Deuteronomy 23:2, KJV)

On Falwell's apparent love of McNuggets: ". . . put a knife to thy throat, if thou [be] a man given to appetite." (Proverbs 23:2, 3, KJV)

Homosexuality: God Hates Fags (and Shrimp Scampi)

Since much of the Bible reflects archaic customs (the blood sacrifice of animals is commanded by God in many scriptures, for instance), deciphering which biblical laws Christians should abide by has become the jurisdiction of theologians and televangelists, the latter group being completely unreliable since they're often stoned from their own hairspray fumes. When faced with troubling or inconvenient laws—like the Bible's promotion of slave owning or its ban on shaving—most evangelicals say, "That's an irrelevant Old Testament–era commandment," and change the subject to activist judges. Still, when the Bible says God finds an act "detestable" or calls something an "abomination," evangelicals insist it must be avoided at all costs. According to most evangelicals, the big abomination is (no shocker here) homosexuality. True to form, evangelicals don't pay attention to some of the other things the Bible designates as being abominable. Most glaringly, Leviticus 11:9–12 says eating shrimp is an abomination:

> 9 . . . whatsoever hath fins and scales in the waters, in the seas, and in the rivers, them shall ye eat.
> 10 And all that have not fins and scales in the seas . . . they shall be an abomination unto you:
> 11 They shall be even an abomination unto you; ye shall not eat of their flesh, but ye shall have their carcases in abomination.

Forget picketing abortion clinics. Head over to Popeye's and Red Lobster! The devil is in the scampi. Evangelicals should be organizing boycotts against Long John Silver's if they want to be consistent. Evidently every person in Maine is going to hell too. Last time we looked, lobsters don't have any fins or scales either.[1]

---

[1] Visit the site that inspired this section, GodHatesShrimp.com, a parody of the inflammatory God Hates Fags Web site of Pastor Fred Phelps. Phelps believes American soldiers in Iraq are being punished by God since the United States is, in his view, too welcoming to homosexuals. Phelps and his followers recently protested funerals of fallen American soldiers. His followers carried inflammatory signs that read "Thank God for IEDs" (improvised explosive devices) and "God Hates Fag Enablers."

 Quick fact: The divorce rate in red states is 27 percent higher than in blue states. Furthermore, born-again Christians have a higher divorce rate than any other social group in the United States.   (U.S. Census Bureau and Barna Research)

James Dobson is too extreme. The biggest threat to the family is people not committing to their relationships, not homosexuality. . . . Being gay isn't a sin, but being promiscuous, whether you're homosexual or heterosexual, is dangerous and not what God wants for anyone's life.

When Did *Evangelical* Become Synonymous with *Pro-Business Republican?*

Pro-business Republicans and evangelicals have been dancing hand in hand ever since they put their patron saint, Ronald Reagan, in office in 1980. It's a counterintuitive alliance, since the pro-business, free-market ideology has systematically bankrupted family farmers, favored CEO bigwigs over blue-collar workers, and supported Wal-Mart's pillaging of small-town America.

Still, founders of the evangelical right, such as Paul Weyrich (p. 159), have been instrumental at mixing a pro-business ideology into the Christian political gumbo. Weyrich is often called the father of the Religious Right. He's also the founder of the Heritage Foundation, a conservative think tank often credited for creating the blueprint for the pro-business, trickle-down tax ideology that has come to define the Republican Party. For decades, pro-business Republicans, such as Weyrich, have systematically been working to attach hot-button pro-family issues (like abortion and gay marriage) to a pro-business platform to help secure the working-class evangelical vote. That is, when they're not spitting on that homeless loser outside of Pier One Imports who's always asking for change.

Many evangelicals also believe that a pro-business, free-market ideology is biblical since several verses in the Old Testament endorse the ownership of private property, private ownership being the foundation of capitalism. Similar to the way liberals interpret the First Amendment to mean *free expression in all forms,* many evangelicals interpret private property to mean *my home, my tax dollars, and my semiautomatic weapon.* Consequently, evangelicals often argue that extraneous taxes and government intervention (i.e., things that inhibit private ownership) defy God's intentions. Socialists beware: to many evangelicals, you're the devil. Ironically, the size of the federal government under the current Republican administration continues to grow faster than you can say *tax cuts are a smokescreen.*

Pro-business Republicans have further enlisted evangelical support by painting liberals as politically correct, immoral elitists who listen to gangster rap. If you listen to Rush Limbaugh, as many evangelicals do, you'd assume that all liberals idolize Michael Moore and want to change the title of the carol "God Rest Ye Merry, Gentlemen" to "Allah, Jesus, Buddha and/or Altruistic Powers of Secular Humanist Love, Rest Ye Merry, Gentlepeople."

And perhaps most significantly, Protestantism began as a protest against the "big government" of the Catholic Church. Martin Luther wanted to express his faith without being stifled by the regulation of a corrupt Church. An aversion to authority, including the government regulation of business and the implementation of taxes, is arguably inherent to Protestantism.

And more tangibly, a pro-business, free-market ideology leads to big savings on diapers and shotguns at Wal-Mart, just like God intended. It's an ideology that looks out for the little guy. Even if the little guy's job was just outsourced to India.

Arguing with Ultraconservative Fundamentalists

Defending the Environment (what they call "Creation Care")

Fundamentalists say: God says in Genesis "let mankind have *dominion* over all the earth." Plus, the Rapture is coming soon, so why bother picking up our beef jerky wrappers if the end is near?

Sinners say: God also promoted *stewardship* of the Earth in Genesis. And dominion isn't a synonym for pillage. Otherwise Genesis would state, "kick the living shit out of that tick-infested dump, it sucks worse than Hell." Environmental disasters, like Katrina or polluted waterways, hit the poor the hardest. In fact, the progressive Christian charity, Christian Aid, released a report in 2006 warning that close to 200 million people could die in Africa by the year 3000 as a result of famine, drought, and floods brought on by climate change. And remember, Revelation 11:18 says God will destroy those who destroy the earth.

GAY MARRIAGE

Fundamentalists say: What's next? Are you gonna let them have sex with cocker spaniels? God calls it an abomination.

Sinners say: Why do evangelicals always use cocker spaniels as an example? Cocker spaniels are *straight*. Greyhounds, on the other hand. Now *they're* into that gay shit. Despite evangelicals' rhetoric about the institution of marriage being placed under attack by the liberals and the gays, the real assault is coming from within their own ranks. According to Barna Research, Born Again Christians have a higher divorce rate than any other social group in the United States.

INTELLIGENT DESIGN

Fundamentalists say: Humans are too complex to not have a Creator.

Sinners say: Who created God? He's complex too, right? Does God have an Intelligent Designer as well? Plus, there are many unintelligent imperfections in nature, such as the human eye, whose inside-out retina causes a blind spot in our field of vision. And come on, would an Intelligent Designer really create Matchbox 20, Vin Diesel, or men with nipples? If you want to teach Intelligent Design, save it for philosophy class. It's not science.

EUTHANASIA

Fundamentalists say: The Youth-in-Asia worship oriental dragon gods and don't realize that the fortunes inside those cookies are tools of Satan.

 Quick fact: "Almost two-thirds of teens (62 percent) believe that the Bible is totally accurate in all of its teachings."

(Barna Group, 2000)

Sinners say: God never intended for us to be kept alive on machines, otherwise he'd have included a power switch on our asses.

MICHAEL MOORE

Fundamentalists say: He's annoying.
Sinners say: He's annoying.

WOMEN

Fundamentalists say: Women need to accept their traditional gender role as casserole-cooking servants. They allowed sin to enter the Garden of Eden and are weaker than men emotionally and physically.

Sinners say: The Old Testament often compares God to a mother. Jesus loved women too. He appeared to Mary Magdalene first after resurrecting instead of revealing himself to some smelly disciple with a fig-leaf jockstrap.

CAPITAL PUNISHMENT

Fundamentalists say: The Bible says *an eye for an eye*.
Sinners say: The Bible also says *thou shall not kill*. Jesus spent his time on earth forgiving and healing sinners, not strapping them to a chair and shooting lightning bolts.

THE IRAQ WAR

Fundamentalists say: We support the troops but often wonder why there was no cool T-shirt line, like in Operation Desert Storm.

Sinners say: We support the troops but wonder why there was no planning or exit strategy.

THE HOLIDAYS

Fundamentalists say: A banner at Target says Happy Holidays! Quick, tell the kids to crouch beneath their desks! There's a war on Christmas!

Sinners say: It's true. We've waged war on the holiday because there is strong evidence to support that Christmas has tried to obtain highly refined aluminum tubes from Africa to reinstate its WMD program. Come on . . . *Nobody*, except Falwell and O'Reilly, cares if you want to call it Christmas or even Baby Jesus Birthday Cake Day. As long as you're okay with Jews wishing you Happy Hanukkah and sending you a Cracker Barrel gift basket where the pork sausage stick has been replaced with Kosher liverwurst, a decorative menorah, and a yarmulke. And incidentally, Bush has sent out a generic "happy holidays" card every year since he's taken office.

FAITH-BASED INITIATIVES

Fundamentalists say: Church-based social services groups should definitely receive government funding, as long as they're not of an immoral non-Christian faith, of course.

Sinners say: People in need of social services and relief should be able to find help without having to visit a government-subsidized group of faith healers who want to convert them and teach them how to handle rattlesnakes. Many "secular" groups have been losing funding to faith-based initiatives, especially if they promote condoms, education about abortion, or break with the evangelical agenda. George Bush even created the White House Office of Faith-Based and Community Initiatives in 2001. And let's be honest, "faith-based" means Christian. Buddhists and Wiccans aren't getting the money to run sex-ed classes and operate homeless shelters.

STEM CELLS

Fundamentalists say: *We couldn't hear what they said . . . it was something inaudibly shrill about babies, the Holocaust, and Ted Kennedy.*

Sinners say: You've got to be kidding. Why not defend the rights of the psoriasis flakes from Pat Robertson's scalp. Or how about boogers?

 Quick fact: "We finally cleaned up public housing in New Orleans. We couldn't do it, but God did."

(Rep. Richard Baker [R-LA] on Katrina, in the *Wall Street Journal*, 2005)

THE POOR

Fundamentalists say: We don't want no welfare nation. Tax-'n'-spend Communists like Howard Dean want to give our money away to the lazy people in society.

Sinners say: The Bible mentions helping the poor over three thousand times. It mentions tax-'n'-spend liberals, um, zero times.

ABSTINENCE EDUCATION

Fundamentalists say: Sex education sends a mixed message. *Virgin* does not mean loser.

Sinners say: Did you wait until marriage? Probably not. And to be clear, *virgin* does, in fact, mean loser. Look it up. (See p. 49 for more on inane abstinence programs.)

ABORTION

Fundamentalists say: You're pro-death, not pro-life.

Sinners say: A member of George Bush's own bioethics team, the neuroscientist and author Michael Gazzaniga, claims that embryos are about as aware as "sea slugs" in their first twenty-six weeks.

BOOZE

Fundamentalists say: God condemns getting drunk.

Sinners say: Jesus's first miracle in John was to turn water into wine for a bunch of drunk people: "Everyone brings out the choice wine first and then the cheaper wine after the guests have had too much to

I just came from a Christian leadership conference and the wine, and beer, and cigars were overflowing. I think that abstaining from those things is what older Christians were concerned with. My parents may have a different view on alcohol, but with me it's not an issue.

drink; but you [Jesus] have saved the best till now." (See how Coors has funded the evangelical right, p. 161.)

(See how Coors has funded the evangelical right, p. 161.)

AFFIRMATIVE ACTION

Fundamentalists say: Minorities don't know how good they've got it here. In fact, they just hired a couple of them coloreds down there at Roy's Discount Muffler Shop. Roy even lets 'em work the cash register when the cameras are turned on!

Sinners say: End affirmative action when equal opportunity *actually exists.*

THE RAPTURE AND END-TIMES

Fundamentalists say: Once the prophecies are fulfilled, Jesus will Rapture the church, just like in that Kirk Cameron movie *Left Behind.*

Sinners say: The word "Rapture" is never once mentioned in the Bible. And with regard to Jesus returning, Matthew 24:36 says, "No one knows about that day or hour." Sometimes we also say, *Are you insane?*

The American Evangelicals

From Pat Robertson to Ralph Reed to the so-called Ten Commandments Judge, Roy Moore, our nation has an abundance of powerful evangelical leaders. Here's our list of the most prominent. Of course we'd like to include a few ultraconservative Catholics as well, like Senator Rick Santorum. After all, Santorum recently blamed the priest molestation scandal on the "moral relativism" that exists in Massachusetts: "Priests, like all of us, are affected by culture . . . it is no surprise that Boston, a seat of academic, political and cultural liberalism in America, lies at the center of the storm." Nevertheless, Catholics like Santorum aren't typically considered to be evangelicals, even when their creepiness rivals that of Pat Robertson. (We've made an exception in chapter 7 with Paul Weyrich, the so-called father of the Religious Right.) Here's our list of the most influential American evangelicals.

ROY MOORE

Ten Commandments Judge

Fire and Brimstone Score: 6

Roy Moore inspires the impressive type of fervor among evangelicals that leads them to urinate on government buildings. Alabama's so-called Ten Commandments Judge caused quite a stir when he defied a court order to have the five-thousand-pound Ten Commandments monument (which he'd commissioned to be built) removed from his courthouse. Protestors camped outside the courthouse for days to protest the removal of "Roy's Rock." When Moore's fan club of Reconstructionist zealots finally left in defeat, "the limestone steps had to be pressure-washed," reports *Atlantic Monthly*, "to remove the smell of urine." Nevertheless, Moore remains a hero among fundamentalists who eat squirrel. Traveling cross-country, often with the monument in the back of a flatbed truck, he's been speaking at conferences, churches, and basically anywhere people with carburetor coffee tables can be found. Moore has political aspirations in Alabama, and many believe he may even run for president. Pretty scary for a man who, according to media reports, used to lead his courtroom in prayer before hearing a case.

Memorable Quote: "Separation of church and state does not mean separation of God and government."

Relevance Today: Alabama polls indicate that people like him.

PHILIP ANSCHUTZ
The Regal Evangelical
Fire and Brimstone Score: 3

Anschutz is the multibillionaire owner of Walden Media, the company responsible for the film *The Lion, the Witch and the Wardrobe* and its sequel, *Prince Caspian*. This ultraconservative Presbyterian is the primary shareholder of Regal Entertainment, the largest movie theater chain in the country. Anschutz also owns the *Washington Examiner* and *San Francisco Examiner*, and has donated hundreds of thousands of dollars to right-wing candidates, antigay groups, and antiabortion groups. According to the Manhattan Institute's *City Journal*, Anschutz fully funded the movie *Ray* and micromanaged the director into toning down some of its drug and sexual content. Ironically, Anschutz was named the nation's "greediest executive" by *Fortune* magazine for cashing out his stock holdings at Qwest Communications before the company took a nosedive. Look for a remake of *Pulp Fiction* at a Regal cinema near you soon. In Anschutz's version, the iconic soundtrack will be revamped with Amy Grant music and the Travolta character will find Christ and begin speaking in tongues during Samuel Jackson's Bible-quoting finale.

Memorable Quote: "We expect them [the movies I produce] to be entertaining, but also to be life affirming and to carry a moral message."

Relevance Today: He's got way too much money to go away.

 Quick fact: Christ is not Jesus's last name. It means "anointed one."

GARY BAUER
The Judas Turtle
Fire and Brimstone Score: 7

There was a time when Gary Bauer was a key evangelical player, but today he's managed to piss off everyone from James Dobson to Pat Robertson to, most likely, Jesus himself. Most people remember one of two things about Bauer: (1) his short-lived presidential run in 2000, which was doomed by allegations of an extramarital affair, or (2) his resemblance to Yertle the Turtle. Nevertheless, Bauer served in the Reagan administration in the eighties, was head of James Dobson's Family Research Council for much of the nineties, and has lived off a diet of walnuts and baby hearts since the seventies. Bauer's rift with the evangelical right accompanied his decision to run for president, a decision that infuriated Family Research Council staffers, who were worried that the move could damage their tax-exempt status. The icing on the cake came after he dropped out of the race and endorsed John McCain—a politician considered soft on abortion and gay rights. Pat Robertson publicly voiced his outrage over the endorsement. Today, Bauer spends most of his time in Dupont Circle, hiding behind a big oak tree, throwing pebbles at gay men, and mumbling under his breath, *"They'll see . . . I hate queers more than Dobson or Robertson!"*

Memorable Quote (Paul Weyrich on Gary Bauer's betrayals of the evangelical right): "May God forgive you, for you know not what you have done."

Relevance Today: Limited, but he's a case study in why John McCain must win over the evangelical right if he wants to run for president. He's the head of the think tank called American Values.

MICHAEL GERSON
The Executive Scribe
Fire and Brimstone Score: 6

It takes divine providence to make George Bush sound presidential. But, before becoming a Bush policy advisor in 2005, it was Michael Gerson's job to do just that. This self-proclaimed evangelical penned many of Bush's sermons—um, we mean speeches—from 1999 to 2004, flavoring each and every one of them with shiny sprinkles of Jesusy goodness. Remember when Bush called the war on terror a "crusade." That was Gerson's word. Or how about the climax of Bush's acceptance speech at the Republican National Convention: "Do you not think an angel rides in the whirlwind and directs this storm?" Gerson again. Nicknamed "the Scribe" by our commander-in-frat-boy, Gerson continues to write many of Bush's important speeches. He admits to inserting religious code words, but says he draws no distinction between quoting from literature and Christian hymns.

Gerson hopes to pen Bush's next State of the Union, where he'll simply encourage Bush to speak in tongues while Benny Hinn performs exorcisms on MoveOn.org liberals. Next, Gerson hopes to be nominated as Bush's Deputy of Inane Nicknames. He could have assuredly come up with something more imaginative than *Brownie*, or *Turd Blossom*, the nickname given to Karl Rove by Bush, given Rove's ability to create positive spin from negative events.

Memorable Quote (on the religious code words in Bush's speeches): "Just because some don't get it doesn't mean it's a plot or a secret."

Relevance Today: Before resigning in 2006, Gerson was highly relevant as part of Bush's inner circle. His impact remains profound. He helped coin the phrase "axis of evil," which set the tone for Bush's *us against them* global policy, and he assisted Bush in nearly all of his important speeches.

JIM BAKKER
The Scandalous Televangelist
Fire and Brimstone Score:
In his prime an 8; he's
more moderate now

Everyone remembers Jim Bakker, the scandal-plagued televangelist whose show *Praise the Lord Club* (PTL) had its heyday in the eighties before he was exposed as a phony. The only thing more scandalous than Jim's notorious affair with buxom Jessica Hahn was his then-wife and cohost, Tammy Faye, who had an equally messy affair with her mascara wand. Before he landed in jail for fraud and conspiracy charges, Bakker's television empire—not to mention his theme park, Heritage USA—amassed a fortune from loyal viewers, affording Bakker several condos, a Rolls, and an air-conditioned doghouse. Today, Bakker is a free man and has his own show once again. Ironically, Tammy has become a gay icon. Jerry Falwell once called Bakker "the greatest scab and cancer on the face of Christianity in two thousand years of church history." Nevertheless, Falwell still holds the title as Christianity's greatest puss-filled cyst.

Interesting fact: Lyndon LaRouche and Jim Bakker were temporarily cellmates during his incarceration.

Relevance Today: None, but his heavily tattooed son has become an influential and progressive "punk" pastor.

PAT ROBERTSON
Pancake Salesman
Fire and Brimstone Score: 8

He sells diet shakes and "Age-Defying Protein Pancakes." We're not joking. That's right, the former presidential candidate, founder of the Christian Broadcasting Network, the Christian Coalition, American Center for Law and Justice, and host of the world's most-watched Christian show, *The 700 Club*, has recently been pawning off age-defying pancakes on the CBN Web site. Now, for a small price, you too can look youthful and vibrant, just like Robertson and the Crypt Keeper! Plus, according to the Web site, Robertson will even provide tips on how to make your pancakes "light and fluffy."

Like Falwell, Robertson has evangelical Tourette's and has managed to offend nearly everyone on Earth, and in Heaven, purgatory, and hell. Everybody has a favorite Pat outburst. Ours occurred when Pat addressed the Republican National Convention in 1992, saying that feminism was "a socialist, antifamily, political movement that encourages women to leave their husbands, kill their children, practice witchcraft, destroy capitalism and become lesbians." His apparent insanity notwithstanding, Robertson's social services charity, Operation Blessing, receives $14.4 million annually in federal funding, under Bush's faith-based initiatives plan. Currently, Pat is working to develop a $60 million biblical theme park on the northern shores of Galilee in Israel called Holy Land Christian Center. Evidently, Christian waterslides have a place in Israel, even if the Palestinians should all be banished, as Pat believes they should. Pat's involvement in the project was put on hold when he suggested that Ariel Sharon's stroke was the judgment of God, infuriating Israeli leaders, who had provided the land for the park free of charge. Pat has since apologized, but many Israeli leaders still think he should be barred from being involved. He should have sent them some pancakes. It's telling of the United States that a man as crazy as Robertson will be remembered as the most important evangelical leader of our time. God help us.

Memorable Quote (*From the CBN Web site*): America loves pancakes! . . . But what are those syrup-drenched hotcakes doing to our bodies? . . . I've created a recipe for Age-Defying Protein Pancakes that will actually give you energy."

Relevance Today: Calling for the assassination of world leaders and blaming 9/11 on gays and the ACLU has made him irrelevant as a front man, but he is still very powerful and influential behind the scenes.

[Pat Robertson] is perhaps too dogmatic in his mind-set for most evangelicals now, but I think he's great. He's been a great example.

Robertson Hall of Fame

On assassinating Venezuelan president Hugo Chavez: "If he thinks we're trying to assassinate him, I think that we really ought to go ahead and do it. It's a whole lot cheaper than starting a war." Robertson later apologized, saying he "spoke in frustration."

On Israel: "I see the rise of Islam to destroy Israel and take the land from the Jews and give East Jerusalem to the Palestinian Authority . . . I see that as Satan's plan to prevent the return of Jesus Christ, the Lord."

On the Pennsylvania school board that shot down teaching Intelligent Design: "If there is a disaster in your area, don't turn to God. You just rejected him from your city."

On gays: "[Homosexuals] want to come into churches and disrupt church services and throw blood all around and try to give people AIDS and spit in the faces of ministers."

On Ariel Sharon's stroke being Divine judgment: "God has 'enmity against those who divide My land.' God considers this land to be His. When you read the Bible, He said this is my land. For any Prime Minister of Israel who decides he will carve it up and give it away, God said, 'No, this is Mine.'"

Pat Robertson! Don't *dare* bring up Robertson!!! For Winter Solstice last year, he promised us Armageddon, but all I got was this lousy NRA membership.

ORAL ROBERTS
900-Foot Bullshitter
Fire and Brimstone Score: 8

Televangelist Oral Roberts never smokes the schwag. The shit he packs in his bong is downright hallucinatory. After all, in 1980 he had a much-publicized vision of a nine-hundred-foot Jesus. He's seen demons and has hosted healing crusades. He says his dad raised a kid from the dead. He used to encourage his viewers to touch the television screen to receive Divine healing. And his Grateful Dead bootleg collection is *extensive*. He's got this awesome all-acoustic set from the Winterland Coliseum in '78 where Jerry bridges a ten-minute version of "Uncle John's Band" into "Dark Star." It's almost as phat as the nine-hundred-foot Jesus.

Memorable Moment: He announced during a fund-raiser that if he didn't raise $8 million for his ministry, God would kill him.

Relevance Today: None. He's as old as Moses, but Oral Roberts University will be his legacy.

HOWARD AHMANSON
Daddy Warbucks
Fire and Brimstone Score: 6

Ahmanson is a millionaire philanthropist and one of the chief funders of the evangelical right. His fat wallet—he inherited a huge fortune from his savings-and-loan tycoon daddy—helped bring the Intelligent Design debate to the American public, since he's the Discovery Institute's (p. 172) primary sugar daddy. Ahmanson regularly siphons money to pro-family groups and helped fund the Bush campaign. He's also linked to an organization called the Chalcedon Foundation, which published literature promoting the stoning of gays. Ahmanson is a known recluse, in part because of his health. He has Tourette's syndrome.

Memorable Quote: Jesus tits! Styrofoam chickencake pagan liberal fuckbiter.

Relevance Today: Very relevant, he's loaded.

Quick fact: Only 56 percent of self-described secularists are registered to vote, whereas 70 percent to 80 percent of Christians in the major Christian denominations are registered.

(Princeton Survey Research Associates, 2001)

JACK CHICK
The Tract-Vangelist
Fire and Brimstone Score: 8

No one knows for sure what he looks like. Some have claimed he's not even a real person. Calls to his office are answered by a friendly assistant who states matter-of-factly that he doesn't do interviews. Nevertheless, *Los Angeles* Magazine reports that he's the most published living author in the world, scaring the bejesus out of children by the millions for decades. The mysterious Jack Chick has good reason to remain incognito. In the past five decades, his pocket-sized, fire-and-brimstone tracts, known as Chick Tracts, have managed to piss off everyone from the Catholics to the Canadian government, who have banned some of his publications. Favorite Chick Tracts topics include the evils of Dungeons & Dragons, razor-blade-stuffed Halloween candy, and how "Jesus is not a fairy." Most climax with an offender, often a child who likes rock music, burning in the fiery abyss. The artwork, which is only occasionally penned by Chick, is unintentionally campy. Chick claims to have gotten the idea to start his own company when he read about Mao Tse-tung's successful use of comics as propaganda in spreading Communism. Today, Chick's work can be found in the Smithsonian Institution but more commonly you can find Chick Tracts at ATM machines and park benches.

Chick Tracts on "devil music": In his tract "Spellbound," Chick's protagonist claims that rock music was created by medieval druids who sacrificed babies to rhythmic drumming. The Beatles "opened up a Pandora's Box when they hit the U.S. with their Druid/rock beat."

Chick Tracts on Catholics and the Holocaust: In "Holocaust," he claims that Nazi death camps were actually orchestrated by the Vatican, who made Hitler their puppet.

Relevance Today: None. He's a campy window into the evangelical old school.

BILLY GRAHAM/FRANKLIN GRAHAM
The Nation's Aging Pastor and his Backward Son
Fire and Brimstone Score: 4 and 7

Billy was friends with Johnny Cash and hangs out with the Clintons. He has a stylish rockabilly hairdo. And he's got a Southern twang that could even charm the cynical disposition of a tax-'n'-spend liberal. It's no wonder people have been waxing nostalgic about our nation's pastor, Billy Graham, who has advised every president since Eisenhower. Even the dumb ones. Graham generally steered clear of the brimstone-and-urine stench that permeates Robertson and Falwell, but his close ties with Nixon jump-started the evangelical right. Despite a polarizing endorsement of George W. Bush, Graham has made a concerted effort to be more inclusive than most of his peers. He recently said Hillary would make a good president. As his legacy ends, his reactionary son Franklin is set to take over his ministry. Evidence of Frankie-boy's ineptitude: he visited Iraq days after we toppled Baghdad to begin converting Muslims, a religion that he has denounced as "very evil and wicked."

Memorable Quote by Billy: "I felt when he [Bill Clinton] left the presidency he should be an evangelist because he has all the gifts and he'd leave his wife to run the country."

Memorable Quote by Franklin: "[H]e certainly did not intend for his comments to be an endorsement for Senator Hillary Clinton. . . . My father, of course, was joking."

Relevance Today: Billy had his "Last Crusade" in 2005, but his son is hoping to return his father's ministry to its backwoods fundamentalist roots.

CHUCK COLSON

The Converted Ex-Con

Fire and Brimstone Score: 6

He once claimed he would trample his grandmother, reports *Slate* of Chuck Colson, to get Nixon reelected. When serving as special counsel to President Nixon, he supported firebombing the Brookings Institution and considered hiring Teamsters to rough up antiwar activists. He was given the nickname "evil genius" by his peers before being sent to jail for Watergate-related crimes. But just prior to being locked away, a magical thing happened to Chuck Colson. He found Jesus. (No, he didn't find Him in the headquarters of the Democratic National Committee that the Nixon administration broke into.) Colson's stint in the joint inspired him to create the faith-based organization Prison Fellowship Ministries, a government-backed program that attempts to rehabilitate jailbirds by converting them. Hundreds of thousands of prisoners have participated. Colson's first novel, *Gideon's Torch*, an antiabortion tome, was published in 1995. The follow-up, *I'd Trample My Grandfather to Get More Faith-Based Initiatives Funded*, is due out sometime before the Rapture.

Memorable Quote: "If we fail to enact a Federal Marriage Amendment, we can expect not just more family breakdown, but also more criminals behind bars and more chaos in our streets."

Relevance Today: Highly relevant. Colson is a White House insider who recently advised Karl Rove on policy in Sudan and is a member of the pro-family lobby the Arlington Group (p. 171).

JERRY FALWELL
The Tourette's-Vangelist
Fire and Brimstone Score: 8

When most people think of the evangelical right, the fundamentalist Baptist reverend Jerry Falwell comes to mind. But Falwell has been discrediting himself for so long, most evangelicals don't even take him seriously anymore. Falwell founded the Christian college Liberty University and that other inconsequential thing called the Moral Majority, the group that started it all. In the seventies, Falwell famously sued Larry Flynt's *Hustler* magazine for running a cartoon parody portraying him losing his virginity to his mother in an outhouse while drunk. (To set the record straight, Falwell wasn't drunk.)[1] Through the years, Falwell has claimed that AIDS is God's wrath on homosexuals, chastised femi-Nazis and the ACLU, and even thinks the purple Teletubbie Tinky Winky is gay. Truth be told, Tinky Winky is straight, though he did experiment in college. Only a town with a name like Lynchburg would claim Falwell as one of their own.

Memorable Quote (on September 11): "I really believe that the pagans, and the abortionists, and the feminists, and the gays and the lesbians who are actively trying to make that an alternative lifestyle, the ACLU, People for the American Way—all of them who have tried to secularize America—I point the finger in their face and say, 'You helped this happen.'"

Relevance Today: Fading, since his health has been declining ever since he got shrapnel in his leg from the war on Christmas. He is still very high-profile at the Hardee's drive-through.

---

[1] He lost the court case, so we can continue to parody him.

LUIS CORTES

Faith-Based Turncoat

Fire and Brimstone Score: 3

Republican, Democrat, Neocon, or Socialist . . . if your candidate needs the support of an evangelical from the Hispanic community, get your checkbook ready, because Luis Cortes is your man. This Philadelphia-based Baptist minister is the founder and president of Nueva Esperanza, Inc., a network of faith-based Hispanic social programs, paid for in part by the Department of Labor. Cortes also established the annual National Hispanic Prayer Breakfast in 2002. Bush routinely attends the event, undoubtedly bungling all attempts at saying *"Como está?"* According to the *New York Times*, Cortes voted for Ralph Nader in 2000, but switched his vote to George W. Bush in 2004 after receiving $10 million in federal contracts from his administration. He takes pride in posing with any candidates who need to prove they care about Hispanics but were turned down by J.Lo for a photo op. Cortes is considered by many to be the most influential Hispanic evangelical in the nation.

Memorable Quote: "This is what I tell politicians . . . you want an endorsement? Give us a check, and you can take a picture of us accepting it."

Relevance Today: A rising evangelical star among Hispanics and white politicians who want to pose for photo ops with one.

 Quick fact: Faith-based funding should be called faith-*biased* funding: 75 percent of Americans support funding Judeo-Christian faith-based initiatives; only 38 percent are in favor of funding Muslim or Buddhist initiatives.

(Princeton Survey Research Associates, 2001)

PAUL CROUCH

TBN's Chief Executive Abomination

Fire and Brimstone Score: 8

When he's not paying hush money to keep homosexual affairs on the down low, Paul Crouch (pronounced *crouch*, not *crotch*) is busy starring on his own Christian variety show, *Praise the Lord*. Crouch is the founder and president of Trinity Broadcasting Network, the world's largest Christian television network. It was revealed in 2004 that Crouch allegedly paid a former employee, Enoch Lonnie Ford, $425,000 to keep his mouth shut in regard to their sweltering, sticky, sinfully sexy tryst of steamy man-love. Crouch's antigay broadcast network has walked away from the scandal relatively unscathed. Still, longtime viewer Earl from Nebraska can't decide if he's more enraged by Crouch's gay affair or by the fact that Enoch Lonnie Ford is "one of them coloreds." Paul and his wife, Jan, are outspoken Pentecostals and have featured shows on their network that include faith healings and exorcisms. The watchdog group Ministry Watch has advised viewers to abstain from giving donations to Trinity's "Praise-a-thons," since they refuse to release financial statements. The watchdog group reports that Trinity has received over $643 million in donations over the last five years. Praise the Lord indeed!

Memorable Quote: "If you have been healed or saved or blessed through TBN and have not contributed . . . you are robbing God and will lose your reward in Heaven."

Relevance Today: His network has a huge audience, despite his extremist Pentecostal opinions, his reputation for greed, and his love of men in hot pants. He's getting old though.

BENNY HINN
Magic Fingers
Fire and Brimstone Score:
N/A—he's exclusively
in it for the money

Hinn is that snazzy faith healer with the Middle Eastern accent, the Jetson's haircut, and the Holy Spirit–exhaust-pipe fingertips that you see on late-night TV. And do you know what? He healed me! Hallelujah. He touched me at a crusade and my body got all tingly. Praise Jehovah. Then he put one of his legs between mine, pushed me, and I fell backward, slain in the spirit. I even skipped my last doctor's appointment, because praise Jesus, I am no longer si— gurgle, ugght, kaplumpt.

Memorable Quote: Claims to be "a new messiah," though people who have refused medical treatment have died after being "healed" by him.

Relevance Today: He healed his way to $89 million in 2002, according to the *Los Angeles Times*, but refuses to make his finances public. He is currently under investigation by the IRS.

WILFORD BRIMLEY
Quaker Oats Guy

Oops. Scratch this one. We got confused for a moment. He's not an evangelical leader. He's just another white man with a big head.

RICHARD LAND

The President's Other Dick

Fire and Brimstone Score: 6

As president of the Southern Baptist Convention's public policy arm, Richard Land is so influential George Bush actually calls *him* to discuss policy. Though sometimes they just discuss how great Michael Landon was on *Highway to Heaven*. Just prior to the invasion of Iraq, Land sent a letter to the president voicing support of the preemptive invasion as being "right and just." It was signed by several top evangelical leaders and was an indirect endorsement by the nation's largest Protestant denomination, given Land's position with the SBC. According to the UK's *Telegraph*, Land even wears a pair of cufflinks, given to him by Bush, that bear the presidential seal. According to PBS's *Frontline*, Land claims that George Bush confided in him before the 2000 presidential election, saying, "I believe that God wants me to be president."

Memorable Quote: "I believe that the United States of America has a divinely given responsibility to hold up the flame of freedom, and whenever possible, to advance it."

Relevance Today: *National Journal* calls Land one of the foremost church-state experts who "politicians will call" about policy.

T. D. JAKES

The Black Billy Graham

Fire and Brimstone Score: 5

The title "The Black Billy Graham" is *Time* magazine's, not ours. We prefer to give him a Batman villain nickname, like "the Babbler," given his frightening habit of speaking in nonsensical tongues. T. D. Jakes is the Pentecostal pastor of The Potter's House in Dallas, Texas, the largest African-American megachurch in the country. (Not to be confused with Harry Potter's House, Hogwarts.) A film based on his bestselling spiritual book *Woman, Thou Are Loosed* was a top-ten film nationwide, he has his own Grammy-winning record label, and his Atlanta-based revival MegaFest attracts over 100,000 people annually. Jakes also wrote a book called *He-Motions* and runs a male empowerment conference called "ManPower," arguably the two gayest titles in the history of Christianity. Homoerotic titles aside, Jakes maintains that gays live a "broken" lifestyle. The multimillionaire pastor preaches a controversial prosperity gospel and owns a $1.7 million home. Just call it the Potter's Mansion. Jakes says he's apolitical but was the keynote speaker at Bush's National Day of Prayer in 2005, and he appeared publicly with Bush in the aftermath of Katrina to help him save face with African Americans.

Memorable Quote: "I wish there were more people like me. The world would be a better place."

Relevance Today: Highly relevant; along with Creflo Dollar, he's the most influential African-American preacher in the country.

JOYCE MEYER
Queen of Televangelists
Fire and Brimstone Score: 5

Joyce Meyer may seem like a token woman on this list, but she's not. She has earned her stripes among the evangelical right's shadiest leaders. No liberal women's-lib promoter, Meyer relied on hard work, dozens of bestselling Christian books, and a closet full of pastel pantsuits from Marshalls to get where she is today. Now the host of her own TV show, Meyer oversees a $90 million-a-year empire. She's proof that a Christian with a lesbian haircut can excel in a secular, male-dominated world. Meyer marches to the beat of her own drum and is known for carrying a purple Bible. Not surprisingly, Jerry Falwell worries that the Bible, like the purple Teletubbie, may be gay. In 2005, the tax-exempt status of her $20 million headquarters in Missouri came under fire, leading to a quiet settlement. According to reports in the *St. Louis Post-Dispatch*, her $900,000 salary, her private jet, and a $30,000 table found on the premises of her ministry's headquarters had raised suspicions about the legality of her tax-exempt ministry.

Memorable Quote: "Make your checks payable to Joyce Meyer Ministries/Life in the Word. And million is spelled M-I-L-L-I-O-N."

Relevance Today: Moderately influential, if she can stay out of jail.

JAY SEKULOW
Jesus's Lawyer
Fire and Brimstone Score: 5

Jay Sekulow is a "Jew for Jesus" who has the ear of the president. Provided, of course, Georgie isn't watching a Transformers marathon on the Cartoon Network. Sekulow is the head of the American Center for Law and Justice (ACLJ, see p. 170), a powerful D.C.-based law firm founded by Pat Robertson to counter the ACLU. Whereas the ACLU—the epitome of evil to most evangelicals—exists to protect the rights of minorities, the disenfranchised, and the powerless, the ACLJ stands up for the rights of that other defenseless class of Americans: white pro-business evangelicals. Sekulow helped draft the Defense of Marriage Act, and in 2005 was intimately involved in Bush's screening process of Supreme Court justices. And when we say *intimate* we mean, yes, he was responsible for giving Bush his daily sponge bath down in the old creek behind the Crawford ranch. Sekulow, who has an uncanny resemblance to *Ghostbuster* Harold Ramis, most assuredly ain't afraid of no ghost. Except the Holy Ghost, of course. Sekulow's also afraid of gay Boy Scout leaders, a scary albeit small demographic who he claims "may well set their sights on your church next." Godspeed, Sekulow. Run! The queer Boy Scout leaders are coming with their homo claws and gayfangs!!

Memorable Quote: "The ACLU clearly has in its agenda the view that, what they call majority religions, Judaism and Christianity in the United States, are the two most likely to be censored and should be censored, in their view."

Relevance Today: A highly relevant Washington insider.

D. JAMES KENNEDY
Evangelical Christianity's
Best-Kept Secret
Fire and Brimstone Score: 7

The Coral Ridge Hour host Dr. D. James Kennedy has been around so long, people just assume he got Raptured years ago. Truth be told, this Fort Lauderdale–based televangelist has been overseeing one of the best-organized conservative grassroots propaganda machines this side of Focus on the Family, known as Coral Ridge Ministries. Kennedy's TV and radio shows have audiences in the millions. Plus, Kennedy hosts an annual "Reclaiming America for Christ" conference to promote Christian theocracy. "As the vice-regents of God," reads literature from the conference, "we are to bring His truth and His will . . . [to] every aspect and institution of human society." Strangely, Kennedy authored a biblical Zodiac book called *The Real Meaning of the Zodiac*, since other interpretations of astrology are, as he says, "a satanic perversion." Sadly he's yet to produce a Christian Ouija board or an evangelical Yogalates workout video. Kennedy's D.C.-based Center for Christian Statesmanship was established to evangelize congressmen, their staffs, and presumably the interns who blow their staffs.

Memorable Quote: "Modern secularists and agnostics do not want to admit that the Christian religion is true, because that would mean that they are sinners; and they have no intention of giving up their right to sin."

Relevance Today: Highly relevant; he has a huge audience and Coral Ridge rakes in $37 million annually.

RALPH REED
Former Golden Boy
Fire and Brimstone Score:
N/A, he seems to have
fallen from grace

He's got the most badass name this side of Lex Luthor but has zero credibility with evangelicals, who think he's become corrupt, given his long list of shady compadres like Jack Abramoff. Reed was a former Bush campaign bigwig and rose to fame as the executive director of Robertson's Christian Coalition. He's always lurking in political shadows somewhere, but sinners, be patient. He's definitely going to hell.

Memorable Quote: "Hey, now that I'm done with the electoral politics, I need to start humping in corporate accounts! I'm counting on you [Jack Abramoff] to help me with some contacts."

Relevance Today: Dwindling

JIMMY SWAGGART
The Pimp Daddy
Fire and Brimstone Score: 8

If televangelist Jimmy Swaggart were to start his career anew, perhaps he'd become a pimp. That way he'd have easy access to the countless prostitutes that checker his scandalous past. After calling Jim Bakker's scandal a "cancer," he got caught with a prostitute, prompting his teary confession: "I have sinned against you, my Lord, and I would ask that your precious blood would wash and cleanse every stain." Some Liquid Tide might work better on those kinds of stains, Jimmy.

Memorable Quote: "And I'm gonna be blunt and plain; if one [a gay man] ever looks at me like that, I'm gonna kill him and tell God he died."

Relevance Today: None, though he somehow has a small TV ministry again.

DAVID BARTON
The Theocratic Propagandist
Fire and Brimstone Score: 6

David Barton is the man behind Wall-Builders, an organization promoting Christian "Reconstructionism" to overcome the "myth of separation between church and state." Want to prove that an outraged George Washington chopped down the cherry tree after discovering the story of Noah's Ark was omitted from his district's Nautical History 101 textbook? David Barton is your go-to man. He has a BA from the prestigious Christian Ivy League, Oral Roberts University, and has written countless books arguing that the Founding Fathers would interpret the First Amendment's line "Congress shall make no law respecting an establishment of religion" to mean *Congress shall ignore all versions of the Constitution except the King James version.* Barton recently printed a retraction for questionable quotes attributed to the Founding Fathers found in his writings after being scrutinized for inaccuracies and exaggerations. Barton is currently the cochair of the Texas Republican Party and a Capitol Hill insider.

Memorable Quote: "The Founders believed that only the Godly would understand the unalienable freedoms provided by God."

Relevance Today: Highly relevant, given the endless church-state separation debate and the advent of the Reconstructionist holiday Ten Commandments Day.

It's no coincidence Tony Perkins shares a name with *Psycho* star Anthony Perkins. He's as nutty as they come. President of the Christian activist group the Family Research Council—a political arm of Focus on the Family—Perkins is James Dobson's main lobbyist, his bitch on the Hill.

TONY PERKINS
The Psycho on the Hill
Fire and Brimstone Score: 8

Anthony Perkins as Norman Bates

Played a psycho who ran the Bates Motel.

Was a homosexual.

Attractive, in a boyish sort of way.

Was overshadowed by his mother.

Stabbed a woman to death in the shower.

Poisoned his mother with strychnine.

Tony Perkins as Head of FRC

Is a psycho who runs the Family Research Council.

Is an antigay activist.

Attractive, in an extra-chromosome sort of way.

Is overshadowed by James Dobson

Purchased a mailing list from former KKK Grand Wizard David Duke and called Jesse Helms "the moral conscience of the Senate."

Applauded African churches for turning down millions in AIDS relief that came from the American Episcopal Church, since they have endorsed gay clergy.

Memorable Quote: "I applaud the actions of the African Anglican churches. No amount of silver is worth sacrificing your duty to your congregation and to God."

Relevance Today: Though his own ambitions have been stunted by controversy, FRC remains one of the most important pro-family Christian groups on the Hill.

Wait Wear

HOLY SH!T

Freaky Christian Products

Left Behind: Where'd Everybody Go? **Video** Evangelicals can buy this for their unsaved loved ones who will be left behind after the Rapture. The video explains how to get saved—since the Christians won't be around to explain it—and lets them know that the Antichrist shall soon come to power.

Wait Wear An abstinence-promoting clothing line featuring panties emblazoned with logos like "Chaste Couture" and "Virginity Lane, Exit When Married." Their Web site claims that founder Yvette Thomas "awoke one night from a dream she had about putting simple messages like 'No Vow No Sex' on underwear." The rest is history.

What Would Jesus Eat, The Maker's Diet, Body by God Three bestselling Christian diet and fitness books.

GodPod A solar-powered device similar to the iPod equipped with a full audio version of the Old and New Testament. Its official name is the MegaVoice.

John Tesh Praise at Red Rocks Enough said.

Bible Bars and Testamints Bible Bars are power bars that contain the seven foods recommended in Deuteronomy 8:8—barley, figs, grapes, honey, olive oil, pomegranates, and wheat. Testamints are breath mints individually wrapped with Bible verses on their labels, evidently for heavenly breath.

Yahwear Features shirts with slogans like "Whaazzuuup? me! when He comes," and our personal favorite, a design of Jesus's punctured palm with an accompanying slogan that reads, "Talk to the Hand." The entire Yahwear line comes with the unofficial guarantee that you will get your ass beaten.

Evangelical Hairdos

Amazing Grace

Prayer Warrior

Beatitude

Communion Bowl

Deprogrammer

Hour of Prayer

Jezebel

Kumbayah

Lottie Moon

Prayer Request

The ~~Rachel~~ Ruth

Tabernacle

Biblical Scholar

Quayle

Televangelist Flip

X-Alter

alt.jesus

Deacon

Rock of Ages

Baby Saver

Seaver

Sharpton

Jesus Jock

Backslider

Ted Haggard, the Duke of Haggard

5

The Duke of Haggard
and the Evangelical Vatican

Ted Haggard: The Duke of Haggard

Fire and Brimstone Score: 6

Denomination: "Spirit-filled" charismatic Baptist

Nutshell: The tongues-speaking, demon-believing, pro-business proselytizing megachurch pastor who speaks with George Bush every Monday

Born: 1956 in Indiana

Defining Quote: "I'm a right-wing religious conservative. . . . I joke that the only disagreement I have with George Bush is on what type of truck to drive."

Quick Facts about Ted Haggard, a.k.a. Pastor Ted

- Is senior pastor of Colorado Springs' New Life Church, called the nation's most powerful megachurch by *Harper's*.
- Heads the National Association of Evangelicals (NAE), which boasts a membership of forty-five thousand churches.
- Is a big fan of the curse-free evangelical-friendly film *Napoleon Dynamite* and has a "Vote for Pedro" bumper sticker on his truck.
- A key member of the conservative pro-family lobby the Arlington Group.
- Loves freedom so much, just talking about it makes him all tingly.
- Owns more Ole Glory boxer shorts than *Merle* Haggard.

The Duke of Haggard

A town as Jesusy as Colorado Springs, often called the Evangelical Vatican given its enormous born-again community, needs *more* than its own pope. The Colorado Springs–based Christian radio host James Dobson is already filling those shoes. That's where Ted Haggard comes into play. Pastor Ted's New Life Church, located at the foot of Pike's Peak, a stone's toss away from the U.S. Air Force Academy, boasts over twelve thousand members and is Colorado's largest megachurch. It's the heart of the Evangelical Vatican. It's like the Basilica of Saint Peter in Rome, only with more soccer moms, a larger parking lot, and an architectural aesthetic reminiscent of a Books-a-Million.

As the spiritual center of Colorado Springs, New Life has been deemed the nation's most powerful megachurch. And in a town where there's very little to do—unless you're into sampling spring water, rootin' down by the power lines, or converting teenage goths who play Magic the Gathering—Ted Haggard's church is the Evangelical Vatican's cultural center as well. Ted Haggard is the Duke of Colorado Springs. All hail the Duke of Haggard. Yee Haw!

Quick Facts about New Life Church

- To keep track of the children in their enormous nursery, children are assigned bar code tags.
- Their small group catalog has fifteen hundred small groups, ranging from Praise Aerobics to a Worship Hula group to groups debunking the science of evolution.
- Their Sunday morning praise band has a turntablist, a hundred-person choir, and fog machines to accompany the music.
- The campus has a Starbucks, a bookstore, a small hotel, and Fort Victory—an Old West–themed room for younger children.
- Is yet to draft plans for the New Life Liquor 'n' Lotto store.

Filibustering in Tongues, IMing with Cheney

He may be a spirit-filled charismatic, but Pastor Ted, who looks like a cross between Oliver North and Richie Cunningham, is no backwoods faith healer. This native Indianan is head of the NAE, the nation's largest, 30-million-member evangelical coalition of churches. When

Haggard's not speaking in tongues, he's busy meeting with world leaders, such as Tony Blair, Arlen Specter, and the leaders of Israel. As first reported in *Harper's*, George Bush calls Pastor Ted every Monday morning to discuss policy. Haggard also claims that the bipartisan group of senators, the Gang of 14, e-mails him regularly to ask his opinion on policy. In regard to his role as president of the NAE, "the representative of evangelicalism worldwide," as he calls it, Pastor Ted boasts that there "has never been a piece of legislation that the NAE has tried to get through Congress that they've failed to get." Not too surprising, considering the NAE's president is apparently hanging out in chat rooms with Cheney or IMing with Condi when he's not on a conference call with Bush.

Everything pastor Ted does is very intentional, very calculated . . . he is walking with the grace and the sovereignty of God. New Life Church was the New Age witchcraft capital of the United States before pastor Ted got here. It was a hot spot for demonic activity.

The Pope and the Duke

As James Dobson's strict Nazarene roots and theological Tourette's begin to distance moderate Christians from his increasingly tactless rhetoric, the Evangelical Vatican is poised for a power coup. The younger and more culturally relevant Ted Haggard, empowered as

Quick fact: Faith healer Peter Popoff was the subject of scandal when it was revealed that he was being fed information about his audience members using a hidden earpiece. He'd falsely claimed that his knowledge of audience members' names and ailments was divinely received from God.

head of the NAE, may soon be riding shotgun in the Popemobile. The two are friends, though Haggard is quick to change the subject at the mention of Dobson's name, acknowledging their "different approaches." Nevertheless, in the spirit of *Freddie vs. Jason* and *Alien vs. Predator*, horror movie director Wes Craven is currently in postproduction on the Christian slasher film *Haggard vs. Dobson*.

Free-Market Jesus

Where leaders like Dobson sound like broken records when it comes to their incessant gay bashing, Haggard is more obsessed with patriotism and promoting the biblical basis of free markets. He claims that capitalism is "scriptural" and that a free-market economy based on a Judeo-Christian worldview is what God intended. Evidently, the Sales and Earnings reports of McDonald's and Wal-Mart got slighted when they weren't canonized in the King James Bible. Bizarrely, Haggard and his congregation casually refer to the hundreds of home-based small groups affiliated with New Life as a free-market system. Nevertheless, their small-group system has more bureaucracy than a Hillary-sponsored health care plan. Leadership training and a police background check are required of small group leaders. And at an end-times small group we visited in a congregant's home, a church leader was present to monitor how it was conducted.

QUICK QUIZ: Choose the book *not* written by Pastor Ted.

A. The Jerusalem Diet: The "One Day" Approach to Reach Your Ideal Weight—and Stay There

B. Taking It to the Streets: Transforming Communities Through Prayerwalking

C. Primary Purpose: Making It Hard for People to Go to Hell from Your City

D. Taking It to the Gym: Prayerjogging to Songs by the Doobie Brothers

E. Foolish No More!

[Correct answer: D]

Hagtastic Praise

Despite his attempts to be progressive and hip—he keeps a bowl of Jelly Bellies in his office and recently bought a scooter—Pastor Ted is in many ways a classic holy-rollin' charismatic. He talks casually about the literal presence of demons. He calls Halloween "an evil holiday" and told his congregation to pray that an ice storm would cancel Satan's holiday. He gleams when discussing New Life's large homeschooled population. He describes his wife's "predictability" as an attribute. He speaks angrily about the "homosexual agenda." And his congregation is filled with thousands of "spirit-filled" Christians who jump up and down ecstatically, many speaking in tongues and waving colorful "praise flags" to soft rock during New Life's weekly services. No snakes were visible on the occasions we visited, but it's our suspicion that Haggard keeps a few vipers in well-hidden cages in the cellar, right next to his chest of Led Zeppelin records sealed away for sermons on satanic backward masking.

The Christian Right needs to realize the war is going to be lost on the gay marriage issue and we need to start figuring out better ways to deal with this issue than the way we're dealing with it now. It really angers me the way it's been politicized and used for fund-raising in political campaigns.

In the Prayer Closet: Don't Be Weird

Haggard knows being *too* Pentecostal could affect his public persona. Following increased media attention, he's been coaching his congregation to avoid discussing the voices they hear in their heads. "Don't be weird," he says. "When we're alone, run around, do cartwheels, kiss your enemy, do whatever you want. But when the cameras come on, remember . . . they cannot understand tongues, they cannot understand cartwheels." He's even become reluctant to discuss his own spiritual gifts. "I don't operate *technically* with the gift of tongues," he says. Nevertheless, he does claim to "pray in tongues every day" in his "prayer closet." Despite his desire to be liked, Haggard recently told Barbara Walters, when she backed him into a corner on a TV special about Heaven, that she was going to hell. It was the rare instance when we actually agree with him.

New Life is decorated with enormous sword-toting angel statues

Rambo Jesus

"Freedom for the world / Freedom for a generation / Let us call to every nation, come"

(Lyrics to a praise song sung at New Life Church)

Haggard believes evangelicals seeking a nonviolent God are searching in vain. "If you want a peaceful God," he says, "choose Buddhism." New Life Church is decorated with enormous bronze warrior angels all

 Quick fact: "I'll see you here, there, or in the air"
(A popular evangelical way to close an e-mail, sermon, or letter)

brandishing menacing larger-than-life swords. They're the church emblems. A variety of sword-toting angel miniatures are even sold in the bookstore. With swords drawn for battle, two especially aggressive sculptures known as "The Defender" and "The Reaper" are apt metaphors for Haggard's belief that Jesus is a God of might. "The God of the Bible has never been peaceful," Haggard says. He recently told *Harper's*, "I teach a strong ideology of the use of power, of military might, as a public service." Clearly, he's misguided. If Haggard was truly a progressive he'd realize that today's Jesus and his band of warrior angels carry hand grenades, not swords. What is this, the Middle Ages?

"We are promoting an ideology"

> *"To be tax-exempt . . . an organization . . . may not attempt to influence legislation as a substantial part of its activities and it may not participate at all in campaign activity for or against political candidates."*

> The IRS

As head of New Life Church and the NAE, Haggard, a self-proclaimed religious right-wing Republican, is rather obvious about his goal to influence political legislation. Haggard says the church should be the "central hub" for political debate in every community. Not to mention, judging by his church lobby, have the best caramel Frappuccino. In reality, little debate exists at New Life Church other than whether to define non-right-wingers as "liberal extremists" or "Godless pagans," as Haggard frequently does. On a recent Sunday, Haggard exclaimed, "Liberal tyranny is on its

I'm pro-life but wouldn't vote solely on that issue.

way," just prior to raising the alert level from red to nut job by promoting a church-sponsored terrorism conference taught by local law enforcement officers. On the following Sunday, he boasted about the growing influence of New Life Church and proclaimed victoriously, "We are promoting an ideology," to resounding applause. Judging by the New Life bookstore, which contains books about Newt Gingrich, George Bush, and *Letters to a Young Conservative*, that ideology is Republican.

"I don't know many people," says Haggard, "who have an appreciation for freedom like I do." We know plenty.

QUICK QUIZ: Ted Haggard in Context

Ted's Ideology: Choose which of the following Ted Haggard did *not* say.

A. *On George Bush*: "[He] will be known as the man who stood up to Islamic fundamentalism . . . in another hundred years, in the Islamic world, he'll be viewed as a great liberator."
B. *On Michael Moore's* Fahrenheit 9-11 *being untruthful:* "[He] communicated to American evangelicals that there was a concerted effort to deceive the nation."
C. *On trickle-down economics:* "The more wealthy people you can create in a culture, the more gifts the poor will receive."
D. *On Katrina*: "George Bush doesn't care about black people."

[Correct answer: D]

Black churches are more exciting, you get more pumped up at them. I've been to white churches and you can't feel the Spirit as much. . . . They talk about politics more.

A Tour of the Evangelical Vatican

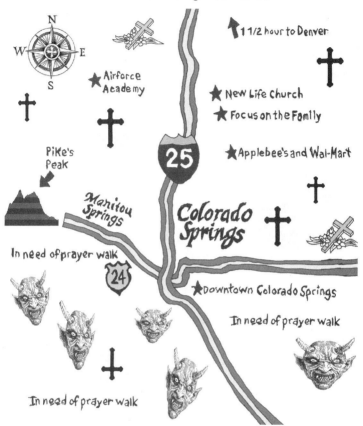

A map of the Evangelical Vatican, Colorado Springs

The Jesus of Colorado Springs

It's fitting that "America the Beautiful" was inspired by the view atop Pike's Peak, the fourteen-thousand-foot snowcapped mountain in Colorado Springs that overlooks the sprawling campuses of Focus on the Family and New Life Church. Aside from Pike's Peak, it's a nondescript mountain town where the clay is red, the people are white, and the sky is blue. Just like Ole Glory. If Jesus had given his Sermon on the Mount atop Pike's Peak, it wouldn't have covered mundane topics like loving your neighbor, helping the poor, and God's enduring love. It would have been about patriotism, the gay assault on the institution of marriage, and the status of the boycott on Disney. The Jesus of Colorado Springs is a white, gun-owning, Velveeta-eating citizen of the United States who buys flag pins for his lapels at Wal-Mart. And the evangelicals you encounter in Colorado Springs want to share the trickle-down economics of His love with you.

As the home of several megachurches and over a hundred religious organizations, including Compassion International, The Navigators, Youth with a Mission, Young Life, International Bible Society, and the Fellowship of Christian Cowboys, Colorado Springs has been officially designated the Evangelical Vatican. It's also the home of the U.S. Air Force Academy, the Pro Rodeo Hall of Fame, and the Museum of the American Cowboy, firmly establishing this mountain town as the capital of the "freedom doesn't come free" T-shirt as well.

Arabs are a cursed people. They're the descendents of Ishmael, who was the adulterous son of Abraham and his handmaid. The Bible says Ishmael was a wild donkey of a man whose descendents would fight with everyone.

God Works in Mysterious Ways. Like Through Neil Bush

Talk to your typical evangelical in Colorado Springs and they'll tell you it was the favor of God that made the air in Colorado Springs lush with the Big Mac–and–baby-powder scent of born-agains. But the truth is, money and a Bush scandal had more to do with the increased presence of evangelicals than God's blessing did.

Before Colorado Springs became known as the Evangelical Vatican, it held the more dubious title of "the forfeiture capital of America," reports the *Globe and Mail*. Back in the eighties, Colorado's

Silverado Banking Savings and Loan was involved in a scandal that cost Colorado taxpayers over a billion dollars. George W. Bush's little brother, Neil, was a director of Silverado Banking at the time. He got off with a $50,000 fine, which was promptly taken care of by a Republican fundraiser. The S&L scandals dragged down land values and dealt a blow to Colorado Springs' economy.

Fearing disaster, Colorado Springs' city council and a local foundation decided to recruit some good Bible-believin' Christian groups with grants and cheap land to help boost their Bushwhacked economy. James Dobson took the bait. He received a $4 million grant and agreed to move his Focus on the Family headquarters from California to Colorado Springs, provided the city council agreed to fumigate first for queers.

Christianity Is Their GNP

Dozens of parachurch groups followed Dobson's lead. The town's population has since grown to nearly fives times its pre–Focus on the Family size. Prefab homes with vinyl siding and electric garage door openers now speckle Colorado Springs' horizon. And the profits at Tootie's Khakis 'n' Stuff Bargain Basement have skyrocketed. Most of the new residents we spoke to claimed to have moved there to escape the "secular" world by working for Christian employers. Many had even started their own Christian ministries and companies. An enthusiastic worshipper at New Life, who wore a jangling charm bracelet filled with tiny fish and a shiny Winnie-the-Pooh miniature, told us she enjoyed all the activities the megachurches offered Christians. "It's like *our* New York," she said, "'cause there's always something to do." The comparison is apt. If you can make it in Colorado Springs for a week, you can make it anywhere. Frighteningly, the evangelicals of Colorado Springs are multiplying like rabbits. According to recent figures, there are two births for every one person who moves there.

Colorado Springs' Christian Business Directory, Some All-Too-Real Highlights

Colorado Springs is so inundated by evangelicals they even have their own 150-page Christian yellow pages. From Christian plumbers to Christian pest control to iRapture, a Christian Web design company, the phone book claims that everyone included has "verbalized their beliefs in Jesus Christ . . . and confessed that He is Lord over their lives, homes, and businesses." Here are some all-too-real highlights from the Colorado Springs 2004–2005 Christian Business Directory:

- **A Christian dentist office** with the pitch "Let the joy of the Lord radiate through your Smile!"
- **All New Innovations Day Spa** provides Christian hair removal, Christian waxing, and Christian Botox.
- **Christian Injury Lawyers** who help "Christians who've been injured."
- A Christian **"Urine Decontamination"** company that claims to be "certified odor specialists."
- **The Pro-Life Real Estate Network** where partial proceeds go toward "pro-life billboards, bus benches, radio ads and television commercials."

Prayerwalking and WD-40

Though Dobson usually gets all the credit for bringing about the evangelical boom in Colorado Springs, the "prayer warriors" at New Life Church tell a different story. In 1984, years before Dobson made the move to the Rockies, pastor Ted Haggard arrived in what he called a "pastors graveyard." Sensing Colorado Springs was overrun by "demonic activity," "humanism," "New Agers," "ex-hippies," and "covens,"

 Quick fact: An estimated 10 percent of all businesses in the United States are "Christian owned and operated," many of which can be found in the Shepherd's Guide, the official Christian business directory. *(Time, September 2005)*

Haggard and members of his church decided to "prayerwalk" the town, reclaiming it for God's purposes, one Applebee's at a time. Haggard and his prayerwalkers visited gay bars, government buildings, and stood outside the houses of "witches," tirelessly chanting and anointing troubled areas with what one New Life congregant described as "gallons of motor oil." Haggard claims his prayerwalking helped transform Colorado Springs into what it is today. He penned a book on the subject called *Taking It to the Streets: Transforming Communities Through Prayerwalking.*

"Pentagrams, ankhs, and bloodied, swollen faces were painted on the walls and ceiling of the old drainage system where we were walking," writes Haggard. "Our flashlight beams barely dispelled the darkness as we inched our way through the maze of tunnels, pipes, and caves that crisscrossed the abandoned mining zone. What was once a bustle of mining activity was now a home for satanic worship."

An early version of the book was titled *The Curse of the Haunted Mining Shaft* and included Haggard being accompanied by the prayerwalking Three Investigators: Bob Andrews, Pete Crenshaw, and Jupiter Jones.

The Force Jesus Academy

The aggressive evangelism taking place in Colorado Springs has begun to meet with some resistance, most vocally from "unsaved" cadets at the Air Force Academy, who are most likely demon-possessed agents of the Dark One who played D&D in their youth. There have been over fifty complaints from cadets who say they've been aggressively proselytized to by evangelical cadets and academy leaders. Several Jewish cadets reported anti-Semitic slurs and alleged they were called "Christ killers" by uniformed cadets. Others confessed that an academy chaplain instructed them to convert their unsaved classmates or "burn in the fires of hell." The scandal hit a fever pitch when the football coach posted a banner that read "Team Jesus Christ." Instead of defending those who feel discriminated against, Ted Haggard and James Dobson have both given high-profile support to the uniformed evangelizers. "The Air Force Academy kids aren't tough enough to talk about God," Haggard mocked, "they need the state to protect them." And when a former Jewish cadet sued the academy for discrimination on behalf of his son, Haggard sent him a taunting e-mail that satirized political correctness. You know, just like Jesus would do.

We Decide to Escape to Downtown Colorado Springs: Addicts, Fiends, and the Jesus Zombies

"Not all who wander are lost"

A bumper sticker spotted in Manitou Springs

Today, most of the godless pagans Haggard expelled with his prayerwalks seem to have relocated to southern Colorado Springs, far away from the born-agains, the McMansions, and the strip malls enveloping New Life Church and Focus on the Family. "Secularists" who don't like iceberg lettuce and American cheese salads tend to live in downtown Colorado Springs. Others live in Manitou, a scenic mountain village filled with springs, cafés, and gift shops that specialize in dreamcatchers and wolf paintings. It's also the part of town one New Life congregant described to us as "the ghetto," apparently because it doesn't have its own Barnes & Noble.

Curiously, a majority of the Christians we came in contact with recommended we avoid Manitou and downtown Colorado Springs altogether in favor of the strip malls. One evangelical told us the downtown was "filled with sex fiends, drunks, and drug addicts." Which, of course, was the perfect endorsement after a few too many visits to the local megachurches.

Unfortunately our ill-advised, vodka-paved tour of the downtown bar district was destined for more evangelizing. As we stumbled out of a popular club that seemed to have a frat-boy-and-date-rape theme,

---

 Quick fact: An evangelical group called Single Focus hosts a weekly Bible study at an Atlanta-based Hooters.

(Associated Press, 2004)

we spotted some fiends, just as we'd been warned. Unfortunately, they weren't sex fiends. They were teenage Jesus fiends, handing out tracts. They seemed frightened, far removed from their usual hangout, most likely the Friendly's north of the city. The small group handed us some literature, which we reluctantly accepted. As we walked away, they told us to check out Hallelujah Night the following week at New Life Church, a Christian alternative to Halloween. "No scary, demonic costumes allowed," they warned. We declined the invitation. We'd already seen enough Jesus zombies at the megachurches we'd attended without having to attend a Christian Halloween party. The tracts they'd handed us read, "If you were to die today, do you know where you'd spend eternity?" Please, God, we thought, don't let it be Colorado Springs.

A Tour of Focus on the Family: Tamela, a Bullet, and Some Stale Dinner Rolls

We completed our trip to the Evangelical Vatican with an obligatory visit to the home of the pope: Dobson's sprawling Focus on the Family office park. The architect of the mountain-draped compound had evidently struggled with the decision on whether to go with an Art Deco look or something more contemporary. He opted for the latter and came up with an elegant Citibank Corporate office meets Six Flags theme.

Focus on the Family's visitors' center has a bookstore with titles like *Really Bad Girls of the Bible*, a movie theater that loops videos of George W. Bush, and a three-story slide for children, positioned just beyond the booths dedicated to Dobson's antiabortion and antigay initiatives. It's all beautifully presented in a series of rooms decorated with airport carpet, fake ivy, and artificial yet well-dusted flowers. And just down the hall, past the gawking Christian tourists from Omaha, there's a trapdoor, constructed in the late 1990s, that leads to the fiery abyss so Dr. Dobson can travel, as he pleases, back and forth from Earth to hell.

To the right of the visitors' center lobby is a room dedicated to the art of G. Harvey, whose paintings are best described as Norman Rockwell meets Hallmark. He's the creator of a series of paintings with names like *A Genteel Nation* and *1600 Pennsylvania Avenue* that feature horse-drawn carriages in front of federal buildings like the White House and the Capitol. Harvey evidently shares Dobson's belief that we should all live in log cabins and read aloud from the Bible to our children after they're done churning the butter for the breakfast flapjacks.

Several times a day, a young woman named Tamela, a wholesome staffer with anchorwoman hair, offers a free tour of the compound and its work cubicles. She tells tourists the history of Focus on the Family, with the climax of the tour being a visit to Dobson's recording studio. Along the way, visitors can see the "Chapelteria," where the staff socializes, prays, and feasts on stale dinner rolls and Pepsi. There's also a bullet that remains lodged in one of their walls, a reminder of a gunman who took four Focus employees hostage. "The gun misfired," Tamela says, informing us that the gunman left without harming anyone. "It was the power of prayer," she said.

At the onset of our fifteen-person tour, Tamela encouraged everyone to introduce themselves. One man from Indiana said he credited Dobson's radio show for George Bush's victory in his state. "Praise God," he said. "Dr. Dobson's ministry rallied the troops and helped us get a victory for Bush." Another couple gushed that they'd been listening to Dr. Dobson every day for fifteen years. This was their Graceland.

I am a firm believer in Intelligent Design. Rainbows, dragons, the Blackened Bowels of Gorgoth: are not these enough to convince the nonbelievers? I.D., as we in the industry call it, is evident on everything from the symmetrical spots on the wings of a butterfly to the evenly spaced thorns on Lucifer's smoldering member.

When Tamela got to us, we told the group we were New Yorkers. We were developing a book about evangelicals. The room became silent. We heard some whispering behind us and feared someone might start coughing to muffle out an epithet like "Satanist" or "Sushi-eater." Tamara lightened the mood with a joke: "Do you all know what a gummy bear really is?" she asked. "It's a bear with no teeth."

A Thorough Debriefing

We'd heard that Dobson and his people run a paranoid ship, and sure enough, after the tour ended we got a thorough debriefing from Dobson's pantsuited PR manager, Gwen Stein. Hearing that the media was in their midst from the Holy Spirit—or perhaps the wholesome staffer with anchorwoman hair—Stein sidled her way in front of one of our reporters, blocking his path to the exit. She had a few questions about the "perspective" of his research. He told her we'd hoped to interview Dobson, but the evangelist wasn't returning our calls. "Dr. Dobson is terribly busy," said Stein. "He generally chooses to do the press that best promotes the beliefs of his ministry." Evidently, those beliefs had something to do with the therapeutic feng shui of airline carpet and artificial ivy, judging by the decor of his compound.

As Stein released our reporter with a pointed "God bless you"—which, like "aloha," means hello *and* good-bye in Christianese—an elderly woman wearing a sweater with an embroidered flower pattern approached us. She had been on the Tamela tour with us and had a voice that reminded us of the Child Catcher in *Chitty Chitty Bang Bang*. Echoing Stein, she inquired, "So what perspective is your book

 Quick fact: California has 178 megachurches, the most of any state, followed by Texas, which has 157.

(Hartford Institute for Religion Research, 2006)

going to be from?" her eyelashes flapping wildly. We were worried she might be demon-possessed.

We responded with a vagary. Told her it was going to be "comprehensive." It wasn't the correct answer. "There are only two perspectives," she snapped. "Christian and not Christian." It was a sentiment we heard often in Colorado Springs.

K&K Mime: Evangelical African-American mimes who perform in white face.

HOLY SH!T

Freaky Christian Ministries

- **K&K Mime:** Two African-American mimes who perform in whiteface. The identical twins, Keith & Karl Edmonds, are the self-proclaimed "founders of gospel mime." "K&K Mime has a burden," claims their Web site, "to reach the people of this present generation, as well as the babes in Christ." Evidently, they've started a trend. The Web site claims that gospel "mime groups [are] popping up all over the place." Visit them at kkmime.com.

- **Holy Land Christian Center:** A $60 million evangelical theme park due to be constructed on the northern shores of the Sea of Galilee in Israel. This pet project of Pat Robertson will cover 120 acres of land given to the project free of charge. Incidentally, Robertson's suggestion that Prime Minister Ariel Sharon's stroke was divine punishment infuriated many Israeli leaders. His involvement has been on thin ice ever since.

- **Canyon Ministries:** Offers a "Christ-centered motorized rafting trip" through the Grand Canyon, where tourists are told the earth is six thousand years old and that the canyon was formed by Noah's flood.

- **Christian Wrestling Federation:** CWF puts the smackdown on the forces of evil. Founded by a spiky-haired, 260-pound former college quarterback who calls himself "Jesus Freak," CWF is a traveling team of wrestlers who have vowed to "wage war with the devil." They stage high-octane matches where muscle-bound wrestlers perform Hulk Hogan–style acrobatics as Christian rock blares from the speakers. Between matches, wrestlers share their Christian testimonies, often with the requisite mention of the biblical battle of David and Goliath. Many of the wrestlers have Christian-themed names like Saint, Angel, Martyr, and Apocalypse. The CWF also runs a training school.

All trainees must agree to attend Bible studies in addition to their time in the ring.

- **Snowflakes:** Nightlight Christian Adoption is not your typical adoption agency. Their program, known as Snowflakes, allows evangelicals to adopt an embryo. Since in-vitro fertilization typically requires the creation of extra embryos, a practice many evangelicals are opposed to, Snowflakes helps ensure that embryos aren't disposed of or used for stem cell research. They call their program Snowflakes since every embryo is different. The company claims that there's no such thing as a "spare embryo," and even have shirts with slogans like "former embryo." An unaffiliated program called Snowflakes Bandits makes a refreshingly minty embryonic smokeless tobacco that sure feels satisfying between your cheek and gum.

- **Josiah Corps:** An organization dedicated to identifying 8–12-year-olds (before they're old enough to be tempted by sin) who have the "divine calling" to be ministers in order to begin training them to do God's work. Founded by George Barna, the go-to Christian statistician for the *New York Times* and most major media organizations. Mr. Barna will still be providing religious statistics for his company, but he claims that mentoring pre-pubeseent children for Godly leadership is the ministry "that really gets [his] juices flowing."

- **Force Ministries:** A ministry composed of Navy SEALs who use skydiving events as an outreach tool for soldiers. An image on their Web site includes a man in army fatigues pointing an automatic weapon beside a caption that reads, "impart faith in Christ."

- **Junkyard Prophets:** A right-wing evangelical rock band that has been touring public high schools. In addition to playing music, the band routinely speaks out against the "evils" of abortion, homosexuality, premarital sex, and gun laws. They charge the typically underfunded schools they visit between $1,500 and $2,500 per performance, money that often comes care of the Department of Education. *The Des-Moines Register* reports that Junkyard Prophets distributed to students overtly religious CDs that stated "[God] declared the death sentence on you due to your sins. . . . When all your sin against God is exposed, how will you escape the damnation of hell?" Equally troubling, an Arkansas newspaper reported that Junkyard Prophets told a group of students that "blaming Columbine on guns is like blaming spoons for Rosie O'Donnell being fat."

- **The Fellowship of Christian Cowboys:** Founded by a rodeo clown and a professional steer wrestler, they use rodeos and Bible camps for evangelism. They even have their own New Testament called "The Way for Cowboys."

- **Surfing the Nations:** An international surfers' ministry targeting Africa, the Middle East, and Central Asia. "Surfing is one of God's modern-day methods to evangelize the world," says their literature. **Snowboard the World** is a related ministry that tries to evangelize to snowboarders. Their Web site proclaims, "Go snowboard . . . into all the world!" Needless to say, they've had limited success in Sri Lanka.

- **The Jesus Hot Air Balloon:** The Merritt Ministry uses hot air balloons for evangelism. They offer rides in a 110-foot balloon designed to look like Jesus sitting on a cloud. Their Web site poses the question, "How do you create a hot air balloon that is both authentic and reverent in its mission?" We really don't know.

- **The Most Bizarre Award Goes to . . . Christian Exodus:** Cory Burnell is moving to South Carolina. Real soon. He's the lollygagging leader of the Christian Exodus, a fundamentalist group intent on making South Carolina a Christian theocracy. Burnell's concept is to have thousands of evangelicals move to the Southern state, and then infiltrate the system by taking low-level government jobs. Once enough Christians relocate and get involved, he believes, a theocracy can be achieved. Ironically, Burnell is yet to make the exodus to South Carolina himself, despite the fact that over a hundred of his followers have already relocated. He's currently living in California. And speaking of irony, isn't South Carolina *already* a theocracy? Burnell has threatened to lead a secession from the Union if needed. That is, if he ever makes it to South Carolina.

Quick fact: A group of lawyers and judges known as the Christian Legal Society, which is backed by Focus on the Family and Campus Crusades among others, was recently organized to defend Christians' right to speak out against gays (and wear T-shirts with antigay slogans) in high schools and on college campuses. They argue it is their Constitutional right to be intolerant. *(Los Angeles Times,* 2006)

Devil Worshippers

Left Behind coauthor Tim LaHaye with the Antichrist and Skeletor

6

Tim LaHate and the
Impending Apocalypse

Timothy LaHaye: The Evangelical Stephen King

Fire and Brimstone Score: 8

Nutshell: Paranoid author of the Christian doomsday series *Left Behind* and conspiratorial avatar of the evangelical right

Denomination: Southern Baptist

Born: 1926

Defining Quote: "I myself have been a forty-five-year student of the satanically inspired, centuries-old conspiracy to use government, education, and media to destroy every vestige of Christianity within our society and establish a new world order. Having read at least fifty books on the Illuminati, I am convinced that it exists and can be blamed for many of man's inhumane actions against his fellow man during the past two hundred years."

Quick Facts about Tim LaHaye

- Coauthor of *Left Behind* books, the series about those left behind to battle the Antichrist after the Rapture. It's sold 62 million copies.
- The Wheaton College School of Evangelical Studies ranks him above Billy Graham, James Dobson, and Pat Robertson as the most influential Christian leader of the past twenty-five years.
- A central architect of the Moral Majority.
- Founder of the Council for National Policy (the evangelical right's Skull and Bones), American Coalition for Traditional Values, and the Pre-Trib Research Center.

- Was college roommates and remains "super close" with Mini Me and Dr. Evil.
- He's not on acid or hallucinogens, as far as we know, but could be stoned from the fumes of the Grecian formula he apparently uses.

The Rise of the Antichrist

59 percent of Americans believe that the End Days prophesied in Revelation will come true.

(Time/CNN Poll, 2002)

Nearly all evangelicals believe that Jesus's Virgin Birth/Water-to-Wine/Nailed-to-a-Cross World Tour was just a precursor to an even larger event depicted in the book of Revelation. Jesus is coming back. And Mel Gibson is already scurrying to obtain the film rights for his sequel to *The Passion of the Christ*. That's right, Jesus had such a shoddy time vacationing on Earth the first time, he's decided it's bound to be better the second time around. Maybe he'll check out the waterslides at Dollyworld or see that Billy Joel musical *Movin' Out* this time.

But before Jesus comes back, most evangelicals believe, the Earth is slotted to become a bad Jerry Bruckheimer movie filled with demons, plagues of locusts, wars, and a career revival for Damien from *The Omen*. And how are evangelicals privy to this esoteric wisdom? The Bible, you say? Oh no. The Bible is indisputably vague about what the End Days will look like and only provides imaginative tales about four-headed beasts and dragons that are open to interpretation. But thankfully, God's apocalyptic plans for the universe are unlocked in Tim LaHaye's *Left Behind* series; books in the series are available for $12.99 at Books-a-Million.

Tim LaHaye is the evangelical Stephen King. His bestselling apoc-

 Quick fact: For decades, Procter & Gamble has been the subject of boycotts by evangelicals. A ridiculous urban myth persists that the company's leaders worship the devil and that their logo incorporates satanic symbols.

alyptic books may be shelved in the action and horror sections at your local library, but the majority of evangelicals believe that the bloody events depicted in the books are accurate representations of how the Apocalypse will unfold. Thanks to Tim LaHaye, millions of evangelicals are convinced the Apocalypse is near. But before the earth goes to hell in a handbasket, they believe, the Rapture will arrive. They'll all ascend into Heaven and meet Jesus in the sky, thanking their lucky stars that they aren't destined to be the characters in LaHaye's books: the left behind.

[Hell is] a place of torment. I think of fire, heat, sulphur, and eternal flame. . . . Some people were chosen [to go to Heaven] before the foundation of the world. Others were predestined to be separated from God, and that's the hard truth of the gospel.

LaHaye's Early Days

The *Left Behind* series, which we will discuss in detail later in this chapter, is just one of many major achievements in LaHaye's paranoia-driven career. In the seventies, LaHaye was an obscure Southern Californian pastor when he founded the religious political lobby known as Californians for Biblical Morality. It was a political coalition of churches emboldened by the desire to fight the *Roe v. Wade* decision, women who wanted equal pay, and a godless culture of miniskirts and rock music. At the time, creating the lobby was a bold move. Religious leaders, like LaHaye's friend Jerry Falwell, worried that Christians wouldn't support churches getting involved in politics. That irksome thingamajig known as the separation of church and state was still held in high regard by many evangelicals.

But LaHaye's coalition had tested the waters for church-based political lobbies, and found them to be warm and not too wavy. So Falwell and LaHaye put on their bathing suits—LaHaye wears a flag thong and

Falwell a '30s-style one-piece—and decided to form the high-profile Christian political machine that started it all: the Moral Majority.

"More than any other person," Falwell told *Rolling Stone*, "Tim La-Haye challenged me to begin thinking through my involvement [in politics]." As head of the Religious Right's first power force, Falwell quickly installed LaHaye on the Moral Majority's board of directors. Still, a more flashy role, like Sin Czar or Condemnation Chieftain, would have been more fitting for a go-getter like LaHaye. (Paul Weyrich also played a pivotal role in the formation of the Religious Right; see p. 159.)

I don't see hell as a literal place with a devil and a pitchfork and fire. I see it as a separation from God and God's love.

Giveth Them Decoder Rings

LaHaye was always paranoid. His "nonfiction" writings expose global conspiracies controlled by secret societies and the little red guy with the pitchfork. He believes, for instance, that the United Nations is the likely predecessor to a Socialist one-world government that will be controlled by the Antichrist. Not surprisingly, LaHaye is also a former member of the anticommunist, Christian political club the John Birch Society. This Cold War–era group believed that the world's governments were being controlled by a conspiratorial cabal of shady politicians and international bankers, not unlike the Bavarian Illuminati or the bad guys in *Lara Croft: Tomb Raider*.

In 1981, LaHaye founded a secretive, ultraconservative political group all his own. It's known as the Council for National Policy (see p. 179). ABC News calls CNP the "Most Powerful Conservative Group You've Never Heard Of." And though their membership list is confidential, George Bush, James Dobson, Bill Frist, Grover Norquist, and dozens of other influential evangelicals have been reported to be members. They even have their own decoder rings, a handshake, and code names like the Falcon, Darth Maul, and the Robot Mangler.

According to reports in the *New York Times*, the influential Council for National Policy has operated behind the scenes for more than two decades, often hosting influential guests like Donald Rumsfeld and Dick Cheney, behind closed doors. All the same, LaHaye's political clout can only thrive in shadows. He still carries the baggage of calling Catholicism "a false religion," was the pastor of a church that published literature referring to Pope Paul VI as the "archpriest of Satan," and was kicked off Jack Kemp's presidential campaign team for his anti-Catholic remarks. Besides, how can you take a man seriously who's written a series of books that are the equivalent of the *Dungeons & Dragons Player's Handbook* for Christians.

Tim "the G Spot" LaHaye

Before penning *Left Behind*, LaHaye published several pseudo-scientific books that blended psychology with biblical instruction. Wheaton College credits LaHaye's early nonfiction books for helping to bring "therapeutic ideas into an evangelical context." Most notably—at least to us—LaHaye coauthored a Christian sex manual with his wife, Beverly, *The Act of Marriage, The Beauty of Sexual Love*. (We wish we were kidding.)

The two lovebirds met while they were students at Bob Jones University, a morally strict fundamentalist college where couples are required to stay six inches apart from each other. They couldn't stay apart for long; the two soon got married and decided that writing a sex guide from the Christian perspective was a good idea. Especially since secular sex books "advocate practices considered improper by biblical standards." Which begs the question, exactly how many pages can you devote to the missionary position?

 Quick fact: True Bethel Baptist Church in Buffalo, New York, may soon get a visit from Jared. They are the first church in the country to have a Subway restaurant inside.

(WVIB News, Buffalo, 2005)

Puzzlingly, the bestselling book cites a study that claims Christian women "experience a higher degree of sexual enjoyment than non-Christians" and are generally "more orgasmic." Who knew? Unfortunately, the guide leaves out the answer to an important question: What should Christians do if they're making love and a premature Rapture occurs? Thankfully, Tim and Bev had the good sense to forgo a scantily clad photo of themselves on the cover.

Not to be outdone by her husband, Beverly LaHaye is the founder and head of Concerned Women for America, which was established in the late seventies to stop ERA. It's essentially the antithesis of the liberal feminist group NOW and functions as a knitting group for self-loathing women who shop at T.J. Maxx. Strangely, despite Tim's decades-long battle to thwart feminism, he's yet to win the battle to keep his own woman at home, barefoot, and pregnant.

QUICK QUIZ: Tim LaHaye is a very prolific author who has written dozens of books in addition to *Left Behind*. Choose the book that Tim LaHaye did *not* author.

A. *Raising Sexually Pure Kids*
B. *The Unhappy Gays*
C. *What Lovemaking Means to a Woman*
D. *Sex Education Is for the Family*
E. *The Queer Queers*
F. *Left Behind: The Kids Series*

[Correct answer: E]

The Unhappy Gays and Other Liter-LaHaye-ture

Though choosing a favorite LaHaye book is a daunting task—he's written over fifty—no LaHaye syllabus could overlook his tome on the "vile" homosexual lifestyle, *The Unhappy Gays*. The out-of-print book expresses his outrage at the term "gay" being co-opted by sodomites to mean something other than *happy*. LaHaye has also written extensively about a medieval pseudo-science known as the four temperaments (in *Spirit-Controlled Temperament* and several other titles), an ancient belief that people's personalities are a reflection of the predominant fluids present in their bodies: blood, phlegm, black bile, or yellow bile. Our guess is that LaHaye is in the black bile camp. And years before he wrote *Left Behind*, LaHaye's *The Battle for the Mind* helped familiarize the American public with the much-maligned epithet for lefties, "secular humanist." It's been a four-letter word among evangelicals ever since.

His Collaborators: Tim's Gang: Jerry Jenkins, Dr. Ice, and *Gil Thorpe*

The only person on planet Earth, apparently, who has written more books than LaHaye is his *Left Behind* coauthor, Jerry Jenkins. Jenkins has written over 150 titles. Jenkins is clearly demon-possessed, or subject to constant floggings by LaHaye, who hovers behind him with a dogsled whip as he types. According to his author bio, Jenkins also authored the syndicated comic *Gil Thorpe* from 1996 to 2004, the noble type of career one would expect from an end-times prophet privy to the Bible's most esoteric wisdom.

LaHaye also collaborates with his partner Dr. Thomas Ice at the Pre-Trib Research Center, an educational institute dedicated to end-times prophecy. When Dr. Ice is not auditioning to be the next Bond villain, he's busy penning end-times reports for the prophecy research center. Their literature states that the two-hundred-member association is made up of the world's top end-times prophecy "scholars." However, we're not sure where their credentials were obtained. The last time we checked, none of the Ivy Leagues like Princeton, Yale, and Harvard offered an Antichrist Studies program.

Bush Almost Left Behind

The Antichrist isn't the only unsavory character with whom LaHaye has been in cahoots. For the past thirty years, LaHaye has spent much of his time here on Earth hobnobbing with the conservative political elite. According to *Rolling Stone*, he was even instrumental in

---

 Quick fact: Almost one-quarter of all Americans believe that 9/11 was predicted in the Bible. (*Time*/CNN Poll, 2004)

---

getting the evangelical right to back George W. Bush prior to his first presidential victory. As chairman of a group known as the Committee to Restore American Values, LaHaye organized a behind-closed-doors session with the then Texas governor, where he was cross-examined by evangelical leaders on issues such as abortion and gun ownership.

At the time, leaders of the evangelical right didn't know what to make of the former party boy, George W. Bush. As evangelical leader and longtime LaHaye buddy Paul Weyrich told *Rolling Stone*, "Bush went into the meeting not totally acceptable. He went out not only acceptable but enthusiastically supported." Evidently, Bush answered all of LaHaye's questions correctly. But the fried crawdaddies Bush sautéed for the gang, in his signature Texas-style tadpole sauce, undoubtedly charmed them as well.

Tim LaHaye in Context

On Jewish conversions after the Rapture: "The Lord will once again deal specifically with the nation of Israel, bringing the Jewish people to faith in Jesus Christ, the Messiah they rejected."

A line from *Left Behind*: "If somebody tried to sell a screenplay about millions of people disappearing, leaving everything but their bodies behind, it would be laughed off."

The Impending Apocalypse

In a country where 59 percent of Americans believe the biblical end-times prophecies depicted in the book of Revelation will come true, LaHaye is the patron saint of Armageddon paranoia. He's popularized the most widely accepted ends-times scenario among evangelicals. But contrary to common misconceptions among sinners, the Apocalypse is more than a great name for a heavy metal band. In the minds of most evangelicals the Rapture is just the beginning. The end-times is actually a complex series of events that will climax with the world's Muslims, Hindus, Zoroastrians, Jews, rock musicians, Buddhists, liberal professors, Atheists, Taoists, Shintoists, Mormons, *New York Times* readers, secular elitists, feminists, and that pagan Gandhi being condemned to an eternal, blood-drenched damnation.

The End-Times According to *Left Behind*

Here's the chronological order of end-times events as depicted by the *Left Behind* series and the movie adaptations starring Kirk Cameron from *Growing Pains*. (Yes, he's on their team now.) It's the predominant view among evangelicals.

1. The Rapture: At some unknowable time in the near future, Jesus will appear to Christians in the clouds. Evangelicals will all immediately be sucked into Heaven, even if they're piloting an airplane full of sinners or ironing a top-dollar monogrammed shirt from Marshalls. Worry not if you get left behind, sinners. Non-Christians will be given a second chance to convert after the Rapture.

2. The Tribulation/Armageddon: After the Rapture, only nonbelievers will be left behind on Earth; 144,000 Jews (the Tribulation Force) will convert to spread Jesus's message. A deceptively charming Antichrist, who is a henchman of Satan, will create a Socialist one-world government and behead Christians who refuse to be tattooed with a 666 bar code. This post-Rapture era, the Tribulation, will last for seven years and will be filled with pestilence, wars, natural disasters, famine, and a resurgence of satanic hair metal bands like Poison and Judas Priest. The Tribulation will climax with Armageddon, a mega-war between the forces of good and evil.

3. The Second Coming/The Millennium: Jesus will return to Earth, slaughter millions of unbelievers, and destroy the Antichrist. The Antichrist's boss, Satan, will be declared an enemy combatant and be imprisoned (Guantanamo Bay may be a good place for him), thus creating peace on Earth. Then, Jesus will set up his kingdom and rule earth for a thousand years. Presumably, he'll be a tax-slaying Republican who will immediately annihilate welfare and appoint Bill O'Reilly as his chief of staff. Oh yeah, midway into the Millennium the Tooth Fairy befriends Santa and Popeye and they create a new holiday where children with clean teeth awaken to a can of spinach beneath their pillows.

4. The Apocalypse: Following the Millennium, Satan is unbound briefly from his captivity. A final apocalyptic battle ensues where Jesus kicks some major demon butt, banishes Satan to hell for all eternity, and destroys the remnants of Earth. Some fringe evangelicals believe

Ronald Reagan will resurrect just prior to Armageddon to slay the entire staff of Moveon.org with the Jesus Sword.

5. Judgment Day: The first day of the rest of your life, when God separates humanity into two distinct camps: Christian Republican Wal-Mart shoppers and Non-Christian Democratic Target shoppers. The former group goes to Heaven. The latter group is sent to an oven, preheated to 650 degrees, for all of eternity. Also, the title of a really horrible Arnold Schwarzenegger movie.

Demon meat is less fatty than beef. It's great for hamburgers.

Other Major Eschatological Beliefs

Note: Eschatology is a fancy word meaning "the study of end-times." Many evangelicals use this scientific-sounding word to convince nonbelievers that they aren't that kooky.

The *Left Behind* view of the Apocalypse is formally known as *Premillennialism*, the belief that the Rapture will occur before the Antichrist comes to power. In other words, evangelicals will be catapulted into Heaven before the shit hits the fan. Here are the other major views:

Postmillennialism Belief that the Rapture will occur following a peaceful Millennium where the world has been almost fully evangelized. Postmillennialists are optimists who believe the world will become more righteous and good before Jesus returns.

Amillennialism Belief that the Millennium (a nonliteral—but long—period of time) is currently under way and that Jesus will eventually return to Rapture his believers into Heaven.

Nehimillennialism Belief that drinking alcohol will be banned during the Millennium, causing Grape Nehi pop to make a comeback.

Is Any of This Rapture Stuff for Real?

Do angels shit in the woods? Of course not. Turns out, the word "Rapture" never even appears in the Bible. John Nelson Darby came up with the concept in the nineteenth century, making the idea pretty, um, infantile, in the context of biblical theology. Plus, as Charles Nelson Reilly of *Hollywood Squares* fame proves, anyone with the middle name Nelson should not be taken seriously.

In more recent times, author Hal Lindsey is credited with popularizing the end-times Rapture craze. His seventies classic, *The Late Great Planet Earth*, sold millions of copies worldwide and was the forerunner to *Left Behind*. The vast majority of LaHaye's eschatological beliefs were shaped by Lindsey's writing, even though most of Lindsey's prophecies—such as his claim in the seventies that Russia was preparing to invade Israel and start World War Three—have largely been discredited. Even Ted Haggard of the National Association of Evangelicals

 Quick fact: In 2005, Republican senator Shelby of Alabama tried to manhandle the Constitution by sponsoring the Constitution Restoration Act, a bill that affirms lawmakers' right to proclaim "God as the sovereign source of law, liberty, [and] government." *(Mother Jones, 2005)*

calls Lindsey "the most consistently wrong man I can think of." We prefer to categorize Lindsey as "the most consistently weird."

Furthermore, the book of Revelation, the primary source material for all biblical end-times prophecy, barely made it into the Bible. Many members of the early church insisted that the book was too muddled to be canonized, and even Martin Luther, the father of Protestantism, insisted the book was not prophetic. Still, LaHaye has managed to create a huge franchise with over a dozen books, films, calendars, and even a $6.50-a-month *Left Behind* prophecy club.

Our Suggestions: Ways to Prepare for Meeting Jesus in the Air, Should the Rapture Arrive

- Get born again and read the complete *Left Behind* series.
- Avoid handcuffing yourself to things.
- Ask the nice Muslim couple down the street to look after the cats.
- Choose a good life insurance plan that provides comprehensive Rapture coverage.
- Hang out in high places, in case the suction on the Rapture vacuum is on the fritz.
- Carry rope, so you can lasso some nonbelievers to bring with you.
- Avoid buying theater tickets in advance, you know, just in case.
- Hire a Jew to drive your car to ensure it won't be unmanned and cause an accident.
- Carry Benadryl, if you get queasy when flying.
- Make sure you're wearing clean underwear.

The Cultural Resonance of Tim LaHate and the *Left Behind* Series

> "[M]en and women soldiers and horses seemed to explode where they stood. It was as if the very words of the Lord had superheated their blood, causing it to burst through their veins and skin. . . . Their innards and entrails gushed to the desert floor, and as those around them turned to run, they too were slain, their blood pooling and rising in the unforgiving brightness of the glory of Christ. . . . Even as they struggled, their own flesh dissolved, their eyes melted and their tongues disintegrated."

> From the final installment of *Left Behind*, *Glorious Appearing*

Given the multitude of evangelicals in this country, it's not surprising that the *Left Behind* books are so successful. Nevertheless, many outsiders to the evangelical right don't realize that an enormous chunk of the population *actually believes* these extraordinarily intolerant books to be an accurate representation of future events. Big deal, right? As we're about to illustrate, the *Left Behind* books are more than benign Christian sci-fi escapism. They're bigoted tirades against anyone who deviates from a conservative evangelical worldview. If a Muslim or a Jew were to write a book that climaxes with the world's Christians being torched with a flamethrower, John Ashcroft would come out of retirement and declare a Christian fatwa against the author.

No Anti-Semitism Left Behind

36 *percent of Americans who support Israel say they do so because they believe Jews must control Israel before Christ can return.*

Time *magazine*

Evangelicals have long been Israel's biggest defenders. It turns out they are largely motivated by their own self-interest. LaHaye and the Premillennialists believe that the Second Coming of Jesus will not occur unless the Jews have sovereign control of Israel. Plus, after the Rapture happens and only sinners are left behind, Premillennialists believe that 144,000 Jews will give into Christmas tree envy and convert to Christianity. So, remaining best buddies with the Israelis is an investment in post-Rapture soul saving for those left behind.

The *Left Behind* books depict all non-Christians being consumed in flames as Jesus rides by on a stallion. They were entertaining books, but I don't agree with how they convey Jesus. That's not the kind of Jesus I believe in.

The Southern Baptist Convention spokesman Richard Land sums up the evangelical position nicely: "We bless the Jews because they are God's chosen people, and God commanded us to, but we also believe that everyone needs to have a personal relationship with Jesus Christ, and we believe that that is true for everyone, including Jews. . . . God promised that land [in Israel] to them."

No Hostility Toward Muslims Left Behind

The *Left Behind* books envision the Jews reclaiming land from the Palestinians to rebuild Jesus's Millennial temple, the place where he will reside after the Second Coming. This all takes place on the site of the Dome of the Rock, an Islamic religious shrine of the highest order. In reality, the thought of Muslims handing over their sacred land to the Jews seems unlikely. But in LaHaye's book *Are We Living in the End Times?*, he suggests a possible solution to this conundrum. The Antichrist, he writes, could intervene and negotiate "an agreement between Israel and the remnants of the Arab world." It's a given in LaHaye's world that Muslims would be willing to make a deal with the Antichrist. After all, they're destined to be Satan's all-star offensive line in hell. It's where they all will be spending eternity.

I look at things like Katrina and Iraq and I don't think they're signs [of the Rapture]. Those kinds of bad things just happen.

No Hostility Toward Catholics Left Behind

Not content to offend non-Christians alone, the *Left Behind* books are also offensive to Catholics. As pointed out by *Salon*, the Antichrist's right-hand man is a cardinal, "all robed and hatted and vested in velvet and piping." So, obviously, he's either a Catholic or Santa Claus. And throughout the first *Left Behind* book, it's stated repetitively that only members of the "true church" get Raptured—the "true church" is a transparent euphemism for Protestants who interpret the Bible literally. Catholics and liberal Christians will presumably be left behind. Most troubling, LaHaye has written that the Roman Catholic Church could likely be the "whore of Babylon," a demonic associate of the Antichrist. It's a shocking assessment given that fact that *everyone* knows the whore of Babylon is Paris Hilton.

I haven't met a lot of people involved in witch-craft, but it takes place. You hear stories, but I've never personally had a confrontation with a witch or a warlock.

No Hostility Toward Liberals Left Behind

> *"One-worlders will not give up until they make the United Nations the ruling force of the world by at least 2025—and maybe sooner!"*
>
> —LaHaye and Jenkins in *Are We Living in the End Times?*

Bizarre fantasy aside, the *Left Behind* books are also outright attacks on what LaHaye calls "secular humanism," a term that is shorthand for *what Ted Kennedy believes.* LaHaye and the Premillennialists believe that the Earth, according to their interpretations of prophecy, *must become more unlivable and increasingly violent* before Jesus can return. Therefore, the efforts of secular humanists who try to preserve

 Quick fact: "A majority of U.S. adults (54 percent) do not think human beings developed from earlier species, up from 46 percent in 1994." (Harris Poll, 2005)

the environment, achieve world peace, or find harmony among the world's religions are not only fruitless, their efforts are literally playing into the devil's hands.

In the *Left Behind* books and elsewhere, LaHaye has documented his belief that a one-world Socialist government run by the Antichrist shall soon come to power. In his paranoid world the United Nations, international treaties, and anything promoting global economies are considered potential predecessors to this one-world government. He claims that he's "opposed the United Nations for fifty years" and uses little subtlety in unleashing his fury against liberals and globalism in the *Left Behind* series.

In the first book of the series, for instance, "pacifist" and "humanist" Nicolae Carpathia mysteriously becomes the secretary-general of the United Nations. Soon after, he's revealed as the Antichrist by the authors. It's no coincidence that LaHaye and his coauthor Jenkins chose a humanist UN leader to be the Antichrist. Did we mention that LaHaye isn't much of a hugger?

No Insanity Left Behind

The cherry atop LaHaye's lunacy sundae is that he believes that the "Satanist" Saddam Hussein could be the forerunner to the Antichrist. In *Are We Living in the End Times?*, LaHaye claims Saddam Hussein received an endowment from a "sun worshipper" in the seventies to rebuild an ancient Babylonian temple close to Baghdad. LaHaye believes this temple will be the future home of the Antichrist. "Saddam Hussein's abnormal hatred for the Jews, Jesus Christ, His followers, and anyone who would stand in the way of his goal to conquer the world," write LaHaye and coauthor Jerry Jenkins, "might best be understood by demonic possession—a virtual foretaste of the Antichrist to follow."

This type of insanity could be ignored if LaHaye wasn't rubbing elbows with important neoconservative policy makers and helping to shape the worldview of millions of evangelicals around the globe. When Hamas rose to power in 2006, LaHaye claimed, "Satan, and radical Islamists, would like nothing better than to thwart the plan of God." An article on the *Left Behind* Web site stated that the "peace can only come through outside intervention," hinting that military intervention in Israel would be acceptable if it could "raise the curtain on the last days."

Facts about the Antichrist 101, According to Tim LaHaye's Book *Are We Living in the End Times?*

- He's likely alive today.
- He's "eastern Mediterranean."
- He is indwelt by Satan and his body is marked with the number 666.
- He's a "thoroughgoing secularist," a "humanist," and a "master diplomat."
- He'll set up a one-world global community, perhaps using the UN.
- He'll reside in a temple in Iraq and amaze with miracles.
- He'll make everyone bear his mark, perhaps through microchip implants in the "fatty tissue behind the ear."
- The mark is "irreversible," and those who have it are doomed to burn in a lake of fire.
- He'll behead those who don't bear his mark and worship him.
- He'll promise world peace, but start World War Three.
- And we can't substantiate it in LaHaye's writings, but we hear that the Antichrist giggles like a schoolgirl when you tickle his feet and is a fervent baker. His creamy scalloped potatoes are yum-mee.

The Growing Pains of the Imminent Apocalypse Doctrine

LaHaye and the Premillennialists have long claimed that Matthew 24:34 holds the key to determining when the End Days will

Quick fact: In 2004, the Bush reelection campaign urged their volunteers to recruit voters from churches. In addition to encouraging them to circulate voter guides at local houses of worship, an official Bush-Cheney reelection document instructed volunteers to obtain church mailing directories and to send them to their local Bush-Cheney reelection headquarters. (*Washington Post*, 2004)

occur. According to their interpretation, the verse prophesies that after Israel becomes a state "a generation shall not pass" before the Lord will come back. Nearly all scholars qualify a biblical generation as being forty years. Yet Israel became a state in 1948, making 1988 the cutoff date for the Second Coming of Christ. Did we miss something or are evangelicals falling behind in math under George Bush's No Child Left Behind program?

Catching their error, most Premillennialists, including LaHaye, have reconsidered their miscalculation. Many now say we should forget the 1948 date and focus on Israel's Six Day War in 1967. Or if that doesn't work out, how about the anniversary of the day Steven Spielberg's first child got bar mitzvahed? He's Jewish, right? Wait a minute. He's a liberal. Scratch that. Now we're all screwed up.

HOLY SH!T

RaptureReady.com

This regularly updated Web site is a handy way to predict the likelihood of the Rapture occurring on any given day. Rapture Ready.com refer to themselves as "The Dow Jones Industrial Average of end time activity." They've made biblical prophecy a precise, quantifiable science.

The site's creators generate what they call "the Rapture Index" by assigning a numerical value to dozens of end-times indicators, such as Inflation, Liberalism, False Christs, Beast Government, Satanism, Interest Rates, Oil Price, Earthquakes, Famine, Plagues, and Globalism. The higher the index number, the more likely the Rapture will occur. In 2005, the Beast Government and Globalism scores were downgraded substantially by RaptureReady.com after the European Union's constitution was voted down. And the False Prophet category rose slightly following the selection of a new pope. At this writing, following an intense hurricane season, unrest in the Middle East, and an unexplained increase in the Web site's Mark of the Beast category, the Rapture Index is at an elevated 154. That's just 28 points behind the record high of 182, which occurred just after September 11. Visit them at RaptureReady.com.

Paul Weyrich, the Evangelical Dr. Strangelove

7

Paul Weyrich and the Vast Right-Wing Conspiracy

Paul Weyrich: The Evangelical Dr. Strangelove

Fire and Brimstone Score: 7

Denomination: Catholic, but so chummy with evangelicals he's accepted as one of their own

Nutshell: The shadowy father of the Religious Right who coined the term *moral majority.*

Born: 1942, Racine, Wisconsin

Defining Quote: "God is indeed a Republican. He must be. His hand helped reelect a president [George W. Bush], with a popular mandate."

Quick Facts about Paul Weyrich

- The founder of the Heritage Foundation, one of the Right's most powerful conservative think tanks, credited for popularizing trickle-down economics in the party.
- Created the Free Congress Foundation, is a founding member of the Council for National Policy, and serves on the executive committee of the Arlington Group.
- Has been in a wheelchair since 2001 because of a spinal injury.
- A frequent political editorialist who enjoys calling Democrats "cultural Marxists."
- Like Dr. Strangelove, has a mechanical arm, which jerks into a heil salute whenever the name Reagan is evoked.

Dr. Strangelove: The Religious Right Is Born

Paul Weyrich is the most important religious leader you've never heard of. Credited with coining the term "moral majority," Weyrich (along with Tim LaHaye) helped convince Jerry Falwell to create an organization to motivate Christian voters. In 1979, while at a Holiday Inn coffee shop with Falwell, Weyrich proclaimed that there was a "moral majority" in America. Falwell liked the phrase so much, he adopted it. And Falwell liked the coffee shop's raspberry-jelly-filled donuts so much, he ordered four and got a tummy ache. Thankfully, Weyrich was there to lovingly hold and burp him.

Known as the Father of the Religious Right, Paul Weyrich is credited with founding several of the organizations responsible for creating "the base" within the Republican Party. Weyrich's Heritage Foundation and Free Congress Foundation helped form the political and religious ideologies, respectively, of the evangelical right. And like the mysterious Dr. Strangelove, Weyrich is a zany wheelchair-bound, neo-fascist political operative, with German heritage and questionable Nazi connections. (See Weyrich's Nazi Connection, p. 162.)

How Weyrich Learned to Start Worrying about
Grassroots and Love the Bong

Back in the late sixties, when the cool kids were busy burning bras, smoking the reefers, and dropping out, the highly religious Paul Weyrich was working as a press secretary for a Republican senator on Capitol Hill. With Lyndon Johnson in office, Weyrich worried that the Right was getting clobbered by the much more politically savvy Democrats, who'd mobilized around civil rights and social activism. (Yes, there was a time

 Quick fact: "Income appears to be inversely related to identifying oneself as a 'born-again Christian.' We found that only 26 percent of those who earn at least $60K a year call themselves born-again, while 44 percent of those who earn under $60K a year identify themselves as born-again Christians." (Barna Group, 2001)

when the Democrats were politically savvy, and yes, Weyrich is the type of ultraconservative who would probably use the word "clobbered.") Weyrich felt the Right was filled with intellectual ideologues more interested in debating political theory than working to get votes.

After attending a Civil Rights Coalition meeting, Weyrich marveled at how organized the grassroots network on the Left was. "For the first time in my life," he told the *Washington Times*, "I saw how they operate." Weyrich decided the Right needed to get serious about organizing its grassroots too. They needed to focus on winning votes. Plus, he *totally* wanted that Jefferson Airplane record the Lefties had been spinning in their smoky chill-out room down the hall from their grassroots meeting.

Other Names Falwell and Weyrich May Have Considered before Deciding to Name Their Organization the Moral Majority

Concerned Milky White Men for America

The Christian Capitalist Club

National Right to Judge Committee

Sin Slayers

God's Love Trickles Down

The Pseudo-Ethical Fringe

The Republichrist Party

Theocracy Now

The Judgmental Activists

The National Jesus and Guns Alliance

The Campaign for Working Snake Handlers

God Hates Carter

People for the American Rapture

The National Donut Alliance

Amazin' Graceroots

The Bloodhound Gang

MoveOn.Borg

The Falwellians

The White Panthers

The Crips

The Silver Bullet

In 1973, six years before the Moral Majority was founded, Paul Weyrich met with Joseph Coors, owner of the Coors Brewing company. The conservative beer mogul had been looking for some pro-business conservative groups to invest in. And, conveniently, Weyrich was eager to begin setting up his own conservative headquarters on a remote desert island and begin hiring robot slaves to assist him in his behind-the-scenes takeover of the sinfully liberal Free World. Weyrich's meeting with Coors was the beginning of a beautiful merger between the religious community and the patron saint of beer, a strange commingling given the anti-alcohol stance of many evangelicals.

Weyrich secured a $250,000 grant from his new barley-and-hops-reeking buddy, and established the Heritage Foundation, the most powerful conservative think tank in modern history. People for the American Way claims Heritage created the "intellectual blueprint" for Reagan's trickle-down economics ideology. You know, the political theory that lower taxes for top-level Republican campaign investors edifies blue-collar workers by providing them with jobs mopping the trickles of urine in their corporate bathrooms. Evidently, trickle-down economics is biblical, since evangelicals are its biggest advocates.

I voted for Bush in 2004 . . . but I also voted for Ken Salazar [a Democrat] when he ran against Pete Coors. I couldn't vote for Coors because I don't like what his company represents. . . . People who drink a lot are not beneficial to society.

Nazi Connection

As pointed out by Joe Conason on *Salon*, Weyrich has a pretty shady past, highlighted by his relationship with Nazi supporters. According to Conason, Weyrich has former political connections to the American Independent Party, which, like the Ku Klux Klan, opposed the Civil Rights movement. More notably, Laszlo Pastor, a convicted World War Two Nazi conspirator, has been identified as an associate of Weyrich's Free Congress. *Salon* reports that Pastor was kicked off the Bush-Quayle campaign for his pro-Nazi entanglements. Weyrich also claims to be an admirer of the isolationist, anti-Semitic radio icon Father Charles Coughlin. And most notably, Weyrich's face partially melted off when he tried to steal the Ark of the Covenant from Indiana Jones on behalf of the Nazi Party.

The Silver Bullet Rides Again

The Heritage Foundation quickly became extremely influential inside the Beltway, but something inside Weyrich's heart of hearts was crying out for more. Sure, the Heritage Foundation was destined to make the rich richer, but Weyrich longed to make the moral moraler, the righteous righteouser, and the secular, well, he wanted them to stop being cretins and buckle up. And yes, Weyrich is the type of guy who would say "cretin" and "buckle up."

Longing to inject a little Jesus into the political landscape, Weyrich resigned from his post as head of Heritage. In 1977, he established the overtly religious Free Congress Foundation (FCF), with another generous grant from Coors. Another conservative think tank, the Free Congress Foundation's stated mission was to avert America's "moral decay" and growing "multiculturalism" by promoting traditional

People who are gay choose to stay that way. If you're a true Christian you won't want to be gay.

"Judeo-Christian" values. In other words, put the gays, liberals, and feminists in a headlock and force them to sing "There Will Be Peace in the Valley" in three-part harmony. FCF became one of the first groups to target evangelicals with direct mailings and recruit Christian activists to get involved in politics.

Groups Coors and the Coors-Owned Castle Rock Foundation Funded, According to People for the American Way

Free Congress Foundation

Morality in Media

Institute for American Values

Institute on Religion and Public Life

Defense Forum Foundation

National Ass. of Christian Educators

Pat Robertson's Regent University

Phyllis Schlafly's Eagle Forum

Institute on Religion and Democracy

Council for National Policy

Promise Keepers

Ethics and Public Policy Center

The Moral Majority

Emboldened by "anti-religion" Supreme Court rulings of the seventies, such as *Roe v. Wade*, not to mention Carter's support of ERA, Weyrich decided the time had come to squash the creeps propagating the liberal agenda. Weyrich's buddy Ed McAteer of the Conservative Caucus convinced Weyrich to organize some creeps of his own.

"McAteer persuaded me," writes Weyrich, "that I needed to

 Quick fact: "The first thing you do is sit down with your wife and say something like: 'Honey, I've made a terrible mistake. I've given you my role. I gave up leading this family, and I forced you to take my place. Now I must reclaim that role.'"

(From the Promise Keepers manifesto
Seven Promises of a Promise Keeper)

I'm definitely pro-life, but I can understand as a woman why someone would have an abortion. I guess I'm confused about this issue . . . hopefully it won't be an issue since I'm waiting until marriage.

meet . . . Jerry Falwell, Pat Robertson, D. James Kennedy, Adrian Rogers, James Robison, W. A. Criswell and many others. In every case I urged them to get active in the political process. They were very reluctant to do so, telling McAteer and me that they were concerned that their followers would cease to support them if they did so. . . . I suggested that we have a professional poll done to determine whether or not it were true. . . ."

A few months later, Weyrich and McAteer arranged a closed-door meeting with all of the aforementioned religious figures to reveal the results of their poll. The overwhelming results of the survey revealed that churchgoers widely supported getting Christian leaders, like Falwell, more involved in the culture wars. "And here was the zinger," writes Weyrich, "the survey showed that people would be willing to contribute [money]. . . . That was it. The Moral Majority was born."

Soon after, with Falwell's rally cry of "get 'em saved, get 'em baptized, get 'em registered," the Moral Majority emerged on the political scene and began recruiting tens of millions of conservative voters from the nation's churches, a practice that continues today. Historians should note, Falwell originally intended to say, "Get 'em saved, get 'em registered, get me some gravy," but decided against it at Weyrich's request.

Paul Needs a Hug

What few know about Paul Weyrich is, despite his bullying of liberals, he's a really sore loser. Weyrich threw a temper tantrum during the Clinton years, writing that the moral majority must be a fantasy, since the American public hadn't booted Clinton out of office. He published an article that encouraged the leaders of the evangelical Reich to simply throw in the towel and drop out of society. Clinton's blow job, "incessant Western rock music," "MTV culture," and political correctness had won the culture war, Weyrich claimed, causing America to slip into "barbarism." Bizarrely, Weyrich said the evangelical Reich should throw out their TVs, consider homeschooling, set up their own "private courts," and disengage from politics.

"We need to drop out of this culture," writes Weyrich, "and find places . . . where we can live godly, righteous and sober lives."

And by sober lives, he of course means enjoying Coors Extra Gold. Predictably, now that Weyrich's team is winning the culture war, he's become highly engaged again. And yes, Weyrich is the type of guy who says stuff like "incessant Western rock music."

Paul Weyrich in Context

On Himself: "My role was basically as coach to the various groups that are now called religious right—to get them to the point where they could function politically and then to put them into a coalition where they could work together."

On FOX News: "Fox News Channel . . . does not purport to have every answer. It merely reports political news from both sides and lets viewers decide."

On Jews: "Christ was crucified by the Jews."

I used to have the utmost respect for the Baptists. I heard their promises of redemption at the river's edge, and I said, "Lucifer's Goat! This is for me." So you can imagine my disappointment when I saw it was a mere two-second dunking. If you really want your sins washed away it takes a good ten- or fifteen-minute submersion. When the sinner stops struggling, the sin's all gone. That's how you know.

The Vast Right-Wing Conspiracy

The Coalitions Cometh Like a Thief in the Night

At the apex of her husband's presidency, Hillary Clinton claimed that there was a "vast right-wing conspiracy." We've come a long way since she made her claim in 1998, but one thing is clear: Right-wingers sure love calling Hillary a lesbian. Truth be told, there is no real vast right-wing conspiracy. Just a lot of powerful, pasty white men who think effeminate guys in biker shorts are putting their marriages at risk. They operate, for the most part, right out in the open.

There may be no conspiracy, but a well-organized machine of right-

 Quick fact: "In 2005, four megachurch pastors were on the *New York Times* bestseller lists."

(Hartford Institute for Religion Research, 2006)

I voted for Bush but don't approve of the Iraq war. I didn't want to change leadership midway through. . . . Neither party is doing enough about health care.

wing evangelicals has been actively mobilizing and growing in clout since the early seventies. Liberals just discounted their efforts since many of their most vocal leaders believe dinosaurs were giant demons that walked the earth at the same time as humans. Meanwhile, this highly organized group of evangelicals and ultraconservatives has helped shift the political landscape of America to the extreme right.

From the overtly evangelical groups like Focus on the Family and Campus Crusades, to politically conservative think tanks like the Heritage Foundation and the American Enterprise Institute, to the supposedly "Fair and Balanced" FOX News network, the organizations promoting an ultraconservative agenda are too many to count. And then there are the church coalitions, most notably the National Association of Evangelicals and the Southern Baptist Convention. The two organizations often function as political lobbies and their leaders discuss policy regularly with the president. Collectively they represent 46 million largely conservative members, most of whom think global warming is something Howard Dean and Al Gore dreamed up in a pot haze at a James Taylor concert.

Beyond the Moral Majority and the Christian Coalition: The Organizations

Falwell's evangelical lobby, the Moral Majority, is defunct. Falwell has been trying to revive the organization with a new name, the Moral Majority Coalition, but a fake war against Christmas notwithstanding, the group no longer has any clout, despite its leader's extensive girth.

Likewise, Pat Robertson's Christian Coalition is all but nonexistent these days. Bad press, lawsuits, and the rising price of Pat's suits at the Burlington Coat Factory have caused their revenues (and reputation) to plummet. At its peak the group was receiving upwards of $26 million annually in revenues, but currently are on the verge of bankruptcy, besieged by creditors' lawsuits and overwhelmed by an estimated $2 million in debt.

Still, there are dozens of vibrant groups marching to the beat of "Onward Christian Soldiers," trying to trademark the name of Jesus for the Republican Party. The following is a list of the dominant right-wing religious and quasi-religious groups who are raising some self-righteous heck in America's political and cultural wars:[1]

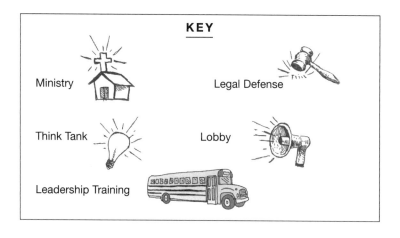

KEY

Ministry

Legal Defense

Think Tank

Lobby

Leadership Training

Alliance Defense Fund The Christian ACLU, defending the "right" to speak in tongues at staff meetings and get gays out of the Boy Scouts. This Christian legal strategy group has funded over

---

[1]Most budget information provided by People for the American Way, a group that is partially responsible for God's vengeance against the United States on September 11, at least according to statements made by Jerry Falwell in 2001 on *The 700 Club*.

thirteen hundred cases. Founders include James Dobson, Rev. D. James Kennedy, and the army of Orcs from *Lord of the Rings*.

Date of founding: 1994   ***Annual Budget:*** $22 million

American Center for Law and Justice Christians hate the ACLU so much, they need two counterweights. The ACLJ is the second. This Christian legal advocacy group was founded by *The 700 Club*'s bobbleheaded mascot, Pat Robertson, who sheds evangelical groups like dandruff flakes. Its leader, Jay Sekulow, was one of the authors of the Defense of Marriage Act. The ACLJ recently defended a group of parents who got a transsexual teacher fired, and a Kmart pharmacist who refused to sell birth control pills to a customer on religious grounds.

Date of founding: 1990   ***Annual Budget:*** $30 million

American Family Association Want to see *Little House on the Prairie* restored to prime time? AFA's got your back. They're the boycott-happy, family-values watchdog trying to control what you watch and hear. They also produced the antihomosexual propaganda video *It's Not Gay*, which ironically is indeed pretty gay. AFA is a very powerful media watchdog, appealing to elderly women who buy Starlight mints in bulk and only watch shows starring Lawrence Welk, Michael Landon, and Angela Lansbury. In 2006, AFA put pressure on NBC to cancel the show *The Book of Daniel* by promising advertiser boycotts and by prompting 700,000 Christians to send complaint e-mails to the network and its affiliates. When the show was canceled, AFA's founder, Don Wildmon, issued a gloating statement, saying, "This shows the average American that he doesn't have to simply sit back and take the trash being offered on TV." Subsequently, AFA pressured NBC into dropping a "sacrilegious" episode of *Will & Grace* that featured Britney Spears as a conservative Christian hosting a cooking show called *Cruci-fixin's*. NBC denies the claims, but nobody believes them.

Date of founding: 1977   ***Annual Budget:*** $11.4 million

> I would never have picked battling porn as my ministry. I struggle with being called the porn pastor. God picked it. . . . I don't want to remove the choice to watch porn, I just want to make a compelling case why not to. I want to say "porn is not all that it's cracked up to be."

Arlington Group A lobby of roughly two dozen religious leaders who meet regularly to discuss policy strategy, with a special emphasis on blocking gay marriage legislation. One of the AG's founders, Paul Weyrich, says the group's inception is "Divine Providence." Members include James Dobson, Ted Haggard, Richard Land, and Gary Bauer. Though they held their first meeting in Arlington, they now meet in D.C., probably at Chili's, where they can discuss ways to ban a woman's right to choose while enjoying an Extreme Poppers with Bacon Basket. A representative from People for the American Way claims Congress's preoccupation with Terry Schiavo in 2005 came primarily as a result of pressure by the Arlington Group.

Date of founding: 2002   *Annual Budget:* Not applicable

Concerned Women for America The antithesis to the National Organization for Women, which is often called the National Organization of Witches by fundamentalists. Its head, Beverly LaHaye (*Left Behind* author Tim LaHaye's wife) thinks feminism is "anti-god, anti-family." Ironically, Bev will probably have to surrender her chairmanship to a man, if CWA ever achieves its goals.

Date of founding: 1979   *Annual Budget:* $12 million

Coral Ridge Ministries The most underestimated grassroots propaganda machine in America. The televangelist and radio host Dr. James Kennedy may not be a household name to most sinners, but his programs reach almost as many people as James Dobson's. His radio program can be heard on 736 stations. His TV program can be seen on 653 stations. Coral Ridge's annual "Reclaiming America for Christ" conference should be renamed "Reclaiming America for Snake Handlers." It assembles all of our nation's top theocracy promoters to snack on pigs in a blanket while they debate who would have pushed harder for a boycott of *The Da Vinci Code*, Jefferson or Lincoln.

Date of founding: 1974   ***Annual Budget:*** $37 million

Discovery Institute Ever wonder why Intelligent Design—the backdoor term being used by Creationists, who argue that a complex universe requires an intelligent creator—has become such a hot-button issue? You can thank this conservative think tank, which has been actively attempting to debunk Darwinism as "just a theory" for over ten years. The bulk of their funding comes from conservative Christians, and, according to the *New York Times*, they have ties to Focus on the Family. Discovery's less-well-known scientific argument, the Limited Intelligence Theory, was recently adopted by a Kansas school board.

Date of founding: 1996   ***Annual Budget:*** $2.5 million

Eagle Forum Phyllis Schlafly established this lobby to battle the Equal Rights Amendment, but it's become an advocate of a grab bag of ultraconservative initiatives. Though it seems like they've been around

Quick fact: "Chances that the divorce of a born-again Christian happened after he or she accepted Christ: 9 in 10."

(*Harper's* magazine, March 2005)

forever, the group is still influential—primarily because Phyllis has name recognition with women who have beehive haircuts and think ladies shouldn't wear jeans. Phyllis needs to wake up and smell the decade, though. The Eagle Forum Web site is encouraging Christians to "demand a continued U.S. defense presence" at the Panama Canal. We'll get on that, Phyllis, right after we're done watching *Rhoda*.

Date of founding: 1972   ***Annual Budget:*** $2.3 million

Ethics and Public Policy Center What would happen if you baptized a gaggle of imperialistic neocons who deify Dick Cheney and Paul Wolfowitz, and forced them to watch 700 hours of *The 700 Club* with their eyes forced open *Clockwork Orange*–style? You'd have the Ethics and Public Policy Center. The International Relations Center calls them "the first neocon institute to break ground in the frontal attack on the secular humanists." In other words, they're a bunch of pro-business, pro-military pod people intent on using religion to justify American imperialism. The group is referred to by name in the book of Revelations as "the pig fuckers of the Apocalypse."

Date of founding: 1976   ***Annual Budget:*** $2.2 million

Family Research Council Set up by James Dobson to serve as a lobbying presence for Focus on the Family on Capitol Hill. FRC is highly influential, and appropriately led by a man named Tony Perkins, who once bought a mailing list from former Ku Klux Klan Grand Wizard David Duke. In Perkins's defense, he doesn't have an affinity for white sheets like the racists at the KKK. His bedsheets have a Chewbacca print.

Date of founding: 1983   ***Annual Budget:*** $10 million

Focus on the Family/Focus on the Family Action The Death Star. Read all about James Dobson's axis of ideology on pp. 2, 6, and 129.

Date of founding: 1977   ***Annual Budget:*** $128 million

Free Congress Research and Education Foundation Paul Weyrich, the Father of the Evangelical Right's home base. Hear him mumbling in his office about activist judges and femi-Nazis when he's not running over the toes of gays with his wheelchair outside Dupont Circle's leather bar.

Date of founding: 1977   **Annual Budget:** $12 million
                                                                        (1997)

Institute on Religion and Democracy The Orwellian Big Brother organization that monitors the activities of "liberal" Protestant churches. The increasingly powerful IRD scrutinizes the activities of "unorthodox" pastors and denomination leaders—the ones who support gays and nonmilitary solutions to world conflicts—and organizes insurrections against them within their own churches by distributing conservative propaganda. When the Episcopal Church endorsed a gay bishop, IRD provided support, and even an office, for a secessionist group opposed to the Church's decision. IRD also launched a vicious attack against churches that "spout pacifist-sounding slogans," claiming America has "a divinely-ordained duty to defend its citizens, by armed force . . . [and] does not require the permission of the United Nations to do so." The IRD has even gone as far as accusing mainline denominations of having an "anti-Jewish animus." The IRD's president, James Tonkowich, is the Karl Rove of the evangelical church, smearing the progress of liberal denomination leaders nationwide. Be careful next time you go to a mainline church. Tonkowich and the IRD may have installed a hidden *gay camera* behind a stack of hymnals.

Date of founding: 1981   **Annual Budget:** $1 million

Leadership Institute They're like a temp agency for people who decorate their homes with the "Footprints in the Sand" plaques. This influential institute has recruited, trained, and provided job placement for over forty thousand "family values" leaders, including Ralph Reed, Grover Norquist, and dozens of congressmen.

Date of founding: 1979   *Annual Budget:* $8 million

 National Council of Churches Oops, they shouldn't be on this list. After all, this coalition of mainline churches often supports nonmilitary solutions to conflicts, affirmative action, working with other faiths, and being more accepting of homosexuals. In other words, they're sinners. In fact, Tim LaHaye claims in *Are We Living in the End Times?* that the National Coalition of Churches is unknowingly fulfilling the goals of the Antichrist by promoting a liberal worldview and by seeking ecumenical solutions to the world's problems.

 National Right to Life Committee and the Pro-Life Groups

- The NRLC is Planned Parenthood's doppelganger. They support the rights of fetuses, stem cells, and brain-dead people being kept alive by machines. Nevertheless, if a brain-dead person being kept alive by machines is on death row, then you can go ahead and kill him. In fact, go ahead and kill the ones on death row with functioning brains too. The NRLC "does not have a position" on *that* Right-to-Life issue.

  Date of founding: 1974   *Annual Budget:* $12 million

- Though they don't have the name recognition as the NCC, the **American Life League** is the largest pro-life educational organization in

---

Quick fact: Two clergy members, one Protestant and one Catholic, sit on the Motion Picture Association of American's board of appeals. They help determine a film's final rating when a director disputes the decision made by the MPAA.

(*Hollywood Reporter*, 2006)

---

the country. Their influence is frightening, considering their Web site claims that rather than use birth control people should trust "in the Lord and His will," since the pill can "kill your baby" and condoms "are potentially harmful."

Date of founding: 1979   ***Annual Budget:*** $7 million

- And then there's **Human Life International**, the international Catholic pro-life lobby working to battle abortion and birth control. One of their more comic studies reports "Christians who use contraceptives . . . seem restless, not at peace with themselves or happy with life." Especially the non–condom users in Africa dying of AIDS, we presume.

Date of founding: 1981   ***Annual Budget:*** unknown

Traditional Values Coalition This multidenominational Christian lobby claims the membership of over forty-three thousand churches. They want prayer in school and Darwin out and have called Democrats "anti-God." Homophobia incarnate, TVC claims that "since homosexual couples can't reproduce, they will simply go after *your* children for seduction." They also say strategies promoting the homosexual agenda are based on "Hitler's writings and propaganda warfare manuals." Which seems logical, since gays love Hitler almost as much as they love Judy Garland. Run, Christians. The impeccably dressed gay neo-Nazi skinheads are coming for the children!

Date of founding: 1980   ***Annual Budget:*** unknown

WallBuilders There's an increasing number of evangelical "Reconstructionists" who believe the Founding Fathers wanted America to be a Christian nation. When they're looking for "historians" to uphold their theocratic beliefs, they often turn to the propaganda videos and literature produced by WallBuilders. Its leader, David Barton, is a Washington insider and cochair of the Texas Republican Party. Republican senator Sam Brownback was moved to tears after watching one of

WallBuilders' videos on the myth of separation of church and state: "I wept thinking how far our nation has moved away from the concepts of the Founding Fathers," he claims. He probably got a little misty watching *Triumph of the Will* too. Nevertheless, WallBuilders is obviously a pack of liars. There's not a single brick mason working at WallBuilders.

Date of founding: 1987   ***Annual Budget:*** unknown

Influential Elements of "the Base"

Christian Colleges: Pat Robertson's Regent University, Jerry Falwell's Liberty University, and Bob Jones University

Christian Broadcasting/News: Pat Robertson's Christian Broadcasting Network, Trinity Broadcasting Network, and Agape Press

Christian Financers: National Christian Foundation, the Scaife Family, Howard and Roberta Ahmanson, the Coors Family

Christian Radio: Salem Communications, Focus on the Family, Coral Ridge Ministries

Christian Motivators: Hillary Clinton, Howard Dean, Michael Moore

Christian Fast Food: Chick-Fil-A and Domino's Pizza (both give money to conservative causes)

Christian Gym: Curves (has given money to pro-life causes)

Surprise Pro-family Donor: The founder and owner of Urban Outfitters and Anthropologie, Richard Hayne, is a conservative who supports pro-family initiatives and gave $13,000 to Senator Rick Santorum.

The Evangelical Illuminati

Okay, Hillary, we take it back. Maybe there is a vast right-wing conspiracy.

The Breakfast Club: The Fellowship

In Arlington, Virginia, overlooking the nation's capital and the scenic Potomac River, there's a $4.4 million mansion, the Cedars, that functions as the secretive homebase of the evangelical right's own secret society, the Fellowship. The group has no business card or Web site, and they've obviously watched too many Al Pacino movies. Members refer to themselves as "the family," and they all share a vow of silence. Yet according to reports in *Harper's*, *Time*, and the *Los Angeles Times*, the Fellowship has been influencing national and international policy for decades. The Fellowship is credited with working on the Camp David Accords, they took part in recent diplomatic talks between Democratic Republic of Congo and Rwanda, and its members routinely travel abroad with policy makers to meet with international leaders.

The group's leader, Douglas Coe, says, "If you want to help people, Jesus said you don't do your alms in public." George H. W. Bush has publicly thanked Coe for his "quiet diplomacy" as an "ambassador of faith." The secretive leader was named one of *Time's* twenty-five most influential evangelicals in 2005.

The Fellowship's largely right-wing membership includes thirty-three members of Congress, including Sam Brownback, James Inhofe, Charles Grassley, Pete Domenici, John Ensign, and Conrad Burns, and has, for over fifty years, been a retreat for world leaders. The Fellowship also owns a multistory town house (zoned as a church) a stone's throw from the Capitol that serves as a home on the Hill to a handful of senators. When asked about the town house, former resident and Congressman Bart Stupak told the *Los Angeles Times*, "We sort of don't talk to the press about the house." He refused to go on the record about the goat's blood, the secret handshake, and the decoder rings too.

Every February, the Fellowship sponsors its annual National Prayer Breakfast, which every president since Eisenhower has attended. Nevertheless, members claim the breakfast is simply a way to recruit new political leaders and Capitol Hill policy makers. Coe says the Fellow-

---

 Quick fact: A fourth of Bush's $15 billion budget to battle AIDS in 2006 was given to faith-based groups, most of which are opposed to education about condoms and safe sex. (Associated Press, 2006)

ship's ultimate goal is to create a "family of friends" and to spread the gospel of Jesus to the world leaders with whom they meet.

Curiously, the Fellowship encourages its members to form small secretive alliances with other members. "The mafia operates like this," their literature reads, according to *Harper's*. "Hitler, Lenin, and many others understood the power of a small core of people." Comparing the group to the mafia, Coe told Fellowship member and Kansas congressman Todd Tiahrt, "For them it's [about] honor . . . for us, it's Jesus."

The Council for National Policy

The Council for National Policy is another highly secretive coalition of evangelicals and politicians. The decades-old group is like Skull and Bones for people who routinely appear on *The 700 Club* or *Hannity & Colmes*. ABC News calls them the "Most Powerful Conservative Group You've Never Heard Of." And though their membership list is confidential, George Bush, James Dobson, Bill Frist, and almost every other A-List ultraconservative who was born again next to the snake cages in the basement of a Baptist church has been reported to be a member.

Major policy decisions often find their inception in the resorts and hotels where the CNP conducts their private meetings. A report by *Rolling Stone* claims that billions have been given to right-wing Christian causes by the CNP, and that the Clinton impeachment was conceived by them. In 2004, the *New York Times* printed an excerpt of a secret CNP document, which instructed: "The media should not know when or where we meet or who takes part in our programs, before or after a meeting." The group's founders include the father of the Religious Right, Paul Weyrich, and Rapture-crazy author Tim LaHaye. Best known for his role on the *He-Man and the Masters of the Universe* television series, Skeletor is another, less widely discussed founder.

HOLY SH!T

Patrick Henry College

Everyone knows that Capitol Hill doesn't have nearly enough out-of-touch, born-again, Aryan policy makers who decorate their offices with guns and Jesus statuettes. A stone's throw from the nation's capital, Patrick Henry College is an evangelical college for aspiring politicians in the business of rectifying this deficit. The *New Yorker* calls Patrick Henry the "Harvard for Homeschoolers," since 85 percent of their students are homeschooled evangelicals with exceptionally high SAT scores. The college provides young conservative Christians with training and, often, internships and job placement in the White House and Congress. Patrick Henry's president claims he started the college, which had its first graduating class in 2004, after receiving numerous requests from congressmen for evangelical interns. Now a high percentage of Patrick Henry graduates have secured staff jobs in Congress and the White House.

Students at Patrick Henry are forced to conform to a dress code, stay out of the dorms of the opposite sex, and avoid any public display of affection. Smoking and drinking are also forbidden. All students must also sign a statement of faith that claims non-Christians will be "confined in conscious torment for eternity." Moreover, Patrick Henry's faculty must agree to teach that creation occurred fully in "six twenty-four-hour days," since this biblical understanding is "the best fit to observed data." Most disturbingly, Patrick Henry's literature claims that the government should be built upon the realization that people "are tainted by sin and therefore cannot be trusted to be free."

"I feel like God wants me to run for president. I can't explain it, but I sense my country is going to need me. Something is going to happen. . . . I know it won't be easy on me or my family, but God wants me to do it."—a quote by George W. Bush, just prior to becoming president.

Rob Bell, the Evangelical Steve Jobs

8

Rob Bell and the Emerging Youth

Rob Bell: The Evangelical Steve Jobs

Fire and Brimstone Score: 2
Denomination: Nondenominational
Nutshell: A Gen X megachurch minister who thinks the evangelical right has got it wrong.
Born: 1970
Defining Quote: "Evangelical conservative Christian faith failed me. It isn't big enough, it isn't inclusive enough, it isn't challenging enough. It doesn't work for me."

Quick Facts about Rob Bell
- Pastor of Mars Hill Bible Church in Grandville, Michigan, which has grown to over ten thousand members since it opened in 1999.
- Says evangelicals like James Dobson are "tragic and toxic" to Christianity.
- Wrote the bestselling religious book *Velvet Elvis: Repainting the Christian Faith.*
- Is a leader of the postmodern, "emerging church" movement.
- *Christianity Today* says Bell puts the "*hip* in disciples*hip*," a designation that, while apt, puts the *dorky* in *dorky.*

Saved by the Bell
Rob Bell thinks Contemporary Christian music is "an abomina-

tion." A thirty-something pastor with Buddy Holly glasses and a Strokes haircut, Bell jokes that the generic Christian music epitomized by Amy Grant and Michael W. Smith almost caused him to fall from grace.

But instead of venturing to the dark side, Rob Bell decided instead to do something about the soulless Christian alternaculture infecting the church. "I grew up playing in bands," says Bell. "I don't relate to a Christian subculture that produces generic, C-minus music and art. . . . It gives Jesus a bad name."

As pastor of Mars Hill Bible Church, Rob Bell wants to make church relevant. Even hip. One of the youngest congregations in the country, Mars Hill is attractive to Gen Xers fed up with churches run by out-of-touch baby boomers. Bell knows that trying to appeal to youth by naming the Friday night service Generation Xtreme is, well, Xtremely retarded.

Bell's church meets in a transformed shopping mall and is crammed to capacity each Sunday with iPod-toting twenty-somethings. During his sermons, Bell name-drops secular bands like Green Day and the Pixies. Insisting that Christians should be creative, much of the music performed at Mars Hill is written by its own members. An artist and author himself, Bell has even produced a series of short evangelical films that address topics like the immediacy of Jesus. One film, called *Rhythm*, features the Chicago Symphony Orchestra performing in a theater while Bell muses on the nature of God.

Bell believes church should be relevant. He recently bypassed the typical altar call by inviting members to come forward to find salvation

I still listen to *some* secular music. That's something I need to work on.

from credit card debt. He made pairs of scissors available at the front of the church for anyone feeling compelled by the Spirit to slice up their MasterCard, AmEx, or Visa.

Pray Different

Bell has more ambitious objectives than being cool. He wants his congregation to rethink their faith. "The word 'evangelical' has been hijacked," he says. "Salvation is something deeper than a list of rules." Bell encourages his congregation to ask the tough questions, like *Does trying to convert people miss the point of the Bible? Does hell exist?* and *Are the Insane Clown Posse really insane or are they demon-possessed?*

Bell is the poster boy of what has become known as the emerging church, an attempt to "disorganize" religion, preach the gospel in fresh ways, and hose down that mothball-and-vinegar stench that Robertson and Dobson have left lingering in the church. Bell's fed up with "tragic and toxic" political ministries like Focus on the Family. He wants evangelicals to have open minds and be creative. He thinks *Left Behind* should be left on the shelf. He hates Contemporary Christian music. Rob Bell wants his congregation to Pray Different. He's the Steve Jobs of Evangelicalism. And he gives us sinners some hope.

Core Beliefs of the Emerging Church Movement
- Question everything you've learned in church, especially if your church has a waterslide.
- Biblical truth is alive and always emerging.
- Jesus probably doesn't want James Dobson performing exorcisms on Ted Kennedy on the Senate floor.

 Quick fact: Generously endowed by ExxonMobil, the George C. Marshall Institute is an influential think tank intent on debunking the science of global warming. Their work has been embraced by science-wary evangelicals and regulations-wary corporations.

(The Republican War on Science, Chris Mooney)

I used to believe we choose God. I don't believe that anymore. God chooses us. There is no free will. You won't find the words "free will" in the Bible. . . . I used to bartend and drink a lot. I used to pick up lots of women. You think I would have given that up on my own? I was having too much fun. God transformed me. I didn't decide to follow God. I was chosen.

- Evangelicals need to reenter culture, instead of creating a generic Xeroxed copy.
- Jars of Clay should be renamed Jars of Suck.
- Evangelicals should loosen up, have a beer, and even say "shit," "dammit," and "friggin'" sometimes.
- *I can't believe I threw my secular CDs away at that Baptist revival in high school.*
- *No, seriously, I really can't believe I did that. I'm a friggin' idiot.*

The Emerging Church

The Emerging Church Movement began in the mid-nineties as a protest against the evangelical right and the over-the-top gimmicks associated with baby-boomer Christianity. Syrupy Christian Rock and atrocities like Bibleman, many felt, had dumbed down the message of Jesus. Pastors such as Bell wanted to find creative ways to make the gospel appealing to young people that had nothing to do with growing goatees or Christian superheroes. Fueled by Web sites and unconventional books written by emerging leaders, the movement began to spread. Especially with young marginalized Christians, who considered U2's *The Unforgettable Fire* an important achievement worthy of canonization.

Today, hundreds of emerging churches meet regularly across the nation—often informally in bars, homes, and coffee shops—to discuss their tattoos, theology, and their stance on being *okay with homosexuality since they used to work with a gay*. Other emerging churches, like Rob Bell's, meet in reconstituted malls, movie theaters, or in sofa-filled sanctuaries often decorated with art created by their own churchgoers. In the era of the megachurch, any place that doesn't look like a baby-boomer church will do. Emerging pastors, like Rob Bell, want to reclaim an attribute that the contemporary church has lost. The sense of being a counterculture.

Unorthodox Quotes from Bell's *Velvet Elvis* that have ticked off Conservatives

- "[S]ometimes when I hear people quote the Bible, I just want to throw up . . . is the Bible the best God can do?"
- "It is possible to make the Bible say whatever we want it to."
- "Anybody is capable of speaking truth. Anybody, from any perspective, from any religion, from anywhere."
- "Litter and pollution are spiritual issues."
- "Salvation is the entire universe being brought back into harmony with its maker."
- "Church is at its best when it is underground, subversive, and countercultural."

The Backdoor Man

Whereas most megachurch pastors are interested in filling chairs, Bell is more interested in getting members *out* of the church. Knowing that Creed and Christian action novels are tools of the Beast, Bell wants his congregation to emerge from the "Christian cocoon" and, well, stop listening to Creed and reading Christian action novels.

Acknowledging his frustration with evangelicals who want to withdraw from the secular world, Bell asks, "If an actor wants to glorify God with his gift, doesn't it make sense for him to do it in a [secular] theater?" Bell says he doesn't "draw a distinction between the sacred and the secular." Nevertheless, Bell thinks evangelicals should set a moral example and probably won't be directing *Pentecostal Girls Gone Wild* anytime soon.

Still, Bell believes that seeking conversions is "the last thing the church should be doing." Instead, evangelicals should be getting involved in their communities and helping people without an agenda. "We've got a really big back door," says Bell, referring to the large number of conservatives who have exited his church in a huff, angry that he's not shoving *convert or burn* clichés down sinners' throats. All the same, having a big back door works well for Mars Hill. Bell would much rather have his congregation glorifying God in their communities, well beyond the walls of the church.

Emerging Answers

Like most members of the Emerging Church Movement, Bell considers himself to be "orthodox," thus breaking with other highly liberal churches (like the Unitarian Universalists, who believe everyone is saved and interpret the Bible very loosely) that are proponents of progressive causes such as gay rights. When asked his opinion on gay marriage, he replied, "I don't have all the answers," a crutch that many emerging pastors fall back on when it comes to controversial topics. After all, in their postmodern worldview, biblical truth isn't formulated. It's "emerging," so dodging tough questions with a well-placed *I dunno, let's talk about God's rainbows* instead is easy. Bell also refused to tell us his opinion on George Bush, and, after some badgering, stated his opposition to a woman's right to choose. These issues notwithstanding, Bell seems to be on the right track. As we said, he hates Plankeye. We're praying for him.

Rob Bell in Context

On Whether Buddhists and Muslims Go to Heaven: "I don't know how all that works, but I do think the gospel is a lot more expansive than the church has acknowledged."

On Mission Work: "You don't go into a Muslim nation in North Africa with a Jesus puppet show. Just help people out without an agenda."

On the Rapture: "The passage people are referring to when they discuss the Rapture is usually in 1 Thessalonians 4, where a Roman emperor is visiting a city that has been crushed by an earthquake. . . . It's a passage about rebuilding and comforting people put on this earth, not about evacuating."

The Emerging Youth

It's not just Michael Moore and fans of *Desperate Housewives* who are fed up with the moral self-righteousness of the evangelical right. Today, an increasing number of young "emerging" Christians, like Rob Bell, have lost patience with James Dobson, the church's obsession with gays and abortion, and the theological value of having a rock-climbing wall inside your church. Some of the evangelical right's most vocal critics are coming from young pastors inside their own ranks.

Emerging pastor **Doug Pagitt** is credited for coining the term "emerging church" at a leadership retreat. The Minneapolis-based pastor also claims "the Constitution allows for a woman to terminate her own pregnancy," and says the Bible's view of homosexuality is "an antiquated, backwater understanding of sexuality."

Jim Bakker's son, **Jay Bakker**, is part of the emerging movement. The "punk rock pastor" touts a motto that "Jesus is the Savior, Not Christianity." He pastors a church in Arizona called Revolution for the city's "counterculture," a group of young artists rejected by the church for their "appearance and lifestyle." Like most members of Revolution, Jay's body is covered with tattoos, lasting stains from Tammy Faye's mascara when he was breast-feeding, no doubt.

Houston-based emerging pastor **Chris Seay** wrote *The Gospel According to Tony Soprano*, after noting parallels between the uber-violent TV mob boss and troubled antiheroes in the Bible. "I remember one night watching Tony Soprano cursing up a blue streak," Seay writes, "as a throng of naked women with near-perfect bodies crowded around him. I flipped over to CNN a few times, but always turned back." The television watchdog American Family Association would be appalled. We're hoping Seay will do a follow-up based on that other

 Quick fact: The Tulsa-based megachurch pastor Carlton Pearson lost 90 percent of his evangelical congregation to an unforgivable scandal: he confessed that he'd stopped believing in hell. *(This American Life, 2005)*

character from the popular HBO series, *The Gospel According to Big Pussy*.

And the emerging movement's informal spokesperson, **Brian McLaren**, is furious over evangelical leaders who "strong-arm" evangelicals into focusing on abortion, gays, and taxes. As pastor of an emerging church in Baltimore and the author of several books, such as *A New Kind of Christian*, Brian was named one of the twenty-five most influential evangelicals in America by *Time*. He says he's a "Post-Protestant" Christian who doesn't need to define himself as an evangelical. "I don't want to give any impression that I want to stay where I'm not wanted," says McLaren. He voted for John Kerry in 2004 and opposed the invasion of Iraq.

Jim Wallis and the Religious Left

In 2005, George Bush visited the evangelical Calvin College in Grand Rapids, Michigan, to deliver a commencement speech. True to form, the Bush administration had been looking for a spot in the state for Bush to deliver a speech before a receptive crowd. Evidently, the Christian college beat out Earl's Discount Body Shop, "home of the Red White and Blue muffler," by a narrow margin. Just prior to the commencement speech, a professor at Calvin surprised many by publishing a letter in the local paper in protest of Bush's visit. Even more surprising, given the college's conservative evangelical credentials, the letter was signed by a third of Calvin's staff and over a hundred members of its student body. Here's an excerpt:

> As Christians we believe your administration has . . . launched an unjust and unjustified war . . . has taken actions that favor the wealthy . . . has fostered intolerance and divisiveness . . . has often failed to listen to those with whom it disagrees . . . [and] we believe your environmental policies have harmed creation.

On the day of Bush's commencement address, approximately a quarter of the student body wore pins attached to their gowns that read "God is not a Republican or a Democrat." Though some of Calvin's less

I thought it was appropriate to invade Iraq in response to 9/11 and as a mission to remove any WMD. Once it was clear that we were not there to get Bin Laden and that there were no weapons of mass destruction, the *real* agenda became clearer . . . that we went to secure our oil interests. I do not think it's appropriate to force a democratic society on a foreign country.

politically inclined undoubtedly stuck with their usual Switchfoot, Amy Grant, and WWJD pins.

"God is not a Republican or a Democrat" has become the anthem cry of Washington, D.C.,–based pastor Jim Wallis, the so-called leader of the evangelical left. The pastor's hugely influential book *God's Politics* is arguably a more important indictment of George Bush than *Fahrenheit 9-11*. Refusing to preach to the choir, *God's Politics* surprised many evangelicals with its fervent criticism of the Iraq war, George Bush, and the evangelical right. Wallis's message to evangelicals is that equating your faith with Bush's preemptive war policy and the divisive goals of the evangelical right is dangerous to Christianity. And as a pastor, Wallis has much more credibility than a knee-jerk liberal like Moore.

Though much more conventional than leaders of the emerging movement, the pastor is the founder of Sojourners and Call to Renewal, two evangelical organizations working to end poverty and promote social activism. Wallis is not exactly a Lefty—he's pro-life and tiptoes around the gay issue—but he's also not trying to force-feed

 Quick fact: In April of 2006, Georgia became the first state to uphold the use of the Bible as a textbook in its public schools. *(The Houston Chronicle, 2006)*

Bibles to people who'd rather be reading a newspaper on Sunday morning than going to church.

Contemporary Christian Music (CCM) and the Christian Cocoon

Jim Wallis and the emerging church have created a slowly spreading ripple in the evangelical baptismal pond. They challenge young evangelicals to question the moral authority of the evangelical right and encourage them to get reengaged in their culture instead of dropping out and forming their own cheesy alternative universe. Nevertheless, a Christian alternaculture equipped with its own movies, paintball parks, nightclubs, tattoo parlors, video games, music festivals, and even its own breath mint (known as Testamints) is growing faster than you can say *Jesus H. Christ*.

Nowhere is this alternaculture more pervasive than in the world of Contemporary Christian Rock, called CCM by evangelicals in the know. The industry has grown upwards of 80 percent in the past ten years and continues to offend the good taste of billions of perplexed sinners annually. Most of the major secular labels even have their own Christian divisions. Andrew Beaujon, the author of *Body Piercing Saved My Life: How Christian Rock Got the Devil's Music to Switch Sides*, says, "As long as born-again parents force their kids to listen to Christian Rock, the industry will continue to grow." It's telling that a large chunk of CCM's core audience initially tunes in *against their will* because their parents won't let them listen to the good stuff. Listening to Christian Rock is a punishment.

From classic stars like Stryper, Carman, Petra, Creed, Steven Curtis Chapman, Phil Keaggy, and Second Chapter of Acts, to the newer favorites like CeCe Winans, Switchfoot, Third Day, POD, Sixpence None the Richer, Jars of Clay, and Kutless, the mind-blowing success of CCM confirms our fears: Satan is alive and well and he's got a hip new haircut. He's destroying the airwaves playing lead guitar in a Christian Rock band.

Horrible Yet Real Contemporary Christian Band and Artist Names

Preachas and Preachas in Disguise

Plankeye

The Revolutionary Army of the Infant Jesus

Savior Machine

Souljahz
Carpenter's Attic
Ace Troubleshooter
10 Cent Offering
Preachas in tha Hood
Gospel Gangstaz
Fighting Instinct
Godrocket
Da Truth
Hangnail
Armageddon Experience
All Saved Freak Band
Brainwash Projects
Eternity Express
The Imitators
Earthsuit
Filet of Soul
Wing and a Prayer

The Preachaholicz
Falling Up
Beneath His Feet
X-Sinner
Phanatik
Acoustic War Against Satan
Pollen Jesus
Neon Cross
Rock N Roll Worship Circus
Inhabited
Armageddon Holocaust
Angel Dust
Children of the Consuming Fire
Hymn Jim
Knights of the Lord's Table
Rap'sures
Oddly Normal
Salvation Air Force

Winner, the Most Horrible Christian Band Name: J.C. Power Outlet

Evangelical Music Festivals, Feigning Evangelical

Each year, over twenty-five thousand young evangelicals attend the music festival known as Cornerstone to hear rehashed Christian Rock music apparently inspired by discarded outtakes from the Stone Temple Pilots. They hide their Marlboros in their backpacks beneath their Bibles and mosh for Jesus. Rock reporter Andrew Beaujon calls Cornerstone "the Hallelujah Palooza." "[I]t's a surprise to see stocked merchandise tables left unattended at night," writes Beaujon. "But if you take away the safe environment, the reasonably priced food and the sober teenage virgins, Cornerstone is a lot like Ozzfest."

Cornerstone is just one of dozens of Christian festivals, including Harvest Crusades, Passion, and the Creation Festival, where Christians by the church-van-ful converge to listen to CCM and repent for breaking their abstinence pledges. Given the slumping sales among "secular" artists, who ironically the Christian artists are ripping off in the first place, some artists are even "feigning evangelical" to boost their sales and be included on the festivals' rosters.

Andrew Beaujon told us that the highly popular Christian band Switchfoot was "freaked out" when he interviewed them at the Cornerstone festival. "They didn't want to be known as a Christian band," says Beaujon, "since that might turn off a secular audience." Beaujon says they were even taken aback when he suggested Cornerstone was a Christian music festival. "They said it wasn't Christian but instead a festival with lots of Christian seekers," says Beaujon. "They've figured out how to have it both ways." Evidently, if you're in the recording industry, getting saved can be very lucrative.

Stephen Baldwin and the Evangelical Skateboarding Ministry

Our favorite evangelical music festival is the Luis Palau Festival. This migratory ministry features live Christian bands and fire-and-brimstone preaching by Luis Palau. On average, it attracts 300,000 to 500,000 people, though the 2005 festival in D.C. nearly got washed out. "I don't know why God would let it rain," said organizer and evangelical minister Luis Palau to a small waterlogged crowd, following a greeting from George W. Bush projected onto large screens behind the stage.

Though dozens of CCM bands are typically booked, the real action at any Luis Palau Festival is the extreme sports. Palau travels with a ten-thousand-square-foot skate park. Dozens of born-again skateboarders and BMX stunt bikers perform stunts for Jesus while born-again host Stephen Baldwin provides testosterone-filled sportscaster commentary that juxtaposes words like "praise" and "hallelujah" with "shredding" and "gnarly." As the crowd cheered thunderously at the

---

 Quick fact: "[Ralph] Reed's public relations and lobbying businesses received $4.2 million from his longtime friend [Jack] Abramoff to mobilize Christian voters to fight the opening of casinos that would compete with Abramoff's Indian tribe clients." (Associated Press, 2006)

2005 festival, Baldwin introduced the bikers and skateboarders, a team of ex-burnout surfer dudes, proclaiming, "[They're] out here representing the Lord." Baldwin's announcement that some of the athletes were also "sponsored by Adidas" was met with a more subdued applause.

Evangelical Raves

"We spin the most kickin' worship tunes," states Club Worship's promotional literature. The Pennsylvania-based club is one of many outreach ministries across the nation devoted to creating a "rave worship" scene devoid of the secular trappings of drugs, sex, and Hello Kitty. (You didn't think it a mere coincidence that Hello Kitty is a mere letter away from being *Hell Kitty*, did you?) Every other Saturday evening, Christian DJs play electronic worship music while young evangelicals with glittery eye shadow and baggy jeans dance, twirl, and "get their praise on" in Club Worship's drug-free environment. They're stoned on God's love, not to mention jacked up on abstinence methamphetamine. The club's founders claim that the heavy bass, the rotating lights, and the urban worship music that kids encounter at Club Worship is "spiritual shock therapy." The club's Web site acknowledges that some evangelicals have criticized their worship methods but insists that God "dances when the backslidden are restored." Even so, God apparently prefers that his followers dance three feet apart, even if they've sworn to remain chaste until marriage. Club Worship "strongly discourages . . . sensual style of dance" or "dancing with a partner." Someone call Kevin Bacon. The prudes at Club Worship need to hear his climactic *Footloose* speech firsthand.

Evangelical Video Games

With politicians such as Hillary Clinton and Joe Lieberman joining forces with the evangelical right to crack down on violent video games like Grand Theft Auto, it's little surprise that there's a growing market for Christian video games. The Christian Game Developers Foundation is a nonprofit evangelical group devoted to promoting guts- and sex-free video games. One title they promote, Left Behind: Eternal Forces, is based on the apocalyptic *Left Behind* novels. A refreshing alternative to violent video games, Eternal Forces promotes a wholesome Christian mythology where a majority of the world's population dies in flame, you know, without all that unneeded violence, sex, and carnage. As the "Left Behind" game's co-creator, Jeffrey Frichner, told the *Los Angeles Times*, "'Left Behind' has the Antichrist, the end of the world, the apocalypse. It's got all the Christian stuff." Evidently, they're not opposed to marketing the same to Satanists as well. Players can elect to role play as the Antichrist and slaughter hapless Christians. Here are a couple of other popular titles endorsed by the Christian Game Developers Foundation:

Catechumen: "Your mentor and brethren have been captured by the demon-possessed Roman soldiers. . . . With your Sword of the Spirit in hand, you must confront the demons head-on and show them nothing can overcome the power of the Holy Spirit. Restore your spiritual health by finding scrolls containing God's Word."

Ominous Horizons: A Paladin's Calling: "Johannes Gutenberg, creator of the printing press, completed his great masterpiece, a printed Bible. . . . With his press destroyed, and the Bible stolen, a Paladin is called upon to once again free the world of evil. . . . You are given three spiritual weapons to aid you: the Sword of the Spirit, the Holy Crossbow and Moses's powerful staff."

Evangelical Action Heroes: Bibleman

Bibleman wants to be the evangelical Superman. But given the inherent cringe factor of his live-action children's show, he's more akin to Barney. Along with VeggieTales, this purple-and-yellow-suited, Bible-quoting superhero has been a staple for evangelical children destined for therapy. Reminiscent of the Power Rangers, Bibleman has his own video series and even tours with his own live theater show. With his "Sword of the Spirit," Bibleman fights off villains including "Luxor Spawndroth," "Gossip Queen," and our favorite, the "Wacky Protestor," an evil liberal intent on creating a world where there are "no Christians, no churches, no Bibles, and no God." Actor Willie Aames (who played Scott Baio's best friend on *Charles in Charge*) is the man in the suit. He was forced to cancel a Bibleman traveling tour in 2001 due to death threats. "We didn't call the FBI but we decided to cancel," Aames told the Columbia News Service. "I got death threats while I was on *Eight Is Enough* [too]." Sounds like the work of Wacky Protestor!

Masturbation is not a great thing in someone's life . . . having impure thoughts about a woman is no different than if you were sleeping with her. I understand why people masturbate, but as a Christian I don't want my penis to be my God.

Typical Coming-of-Age Rituals for Young Evangelicals

1. Commit to Jesus at youth group, a Christian concert, or in biology class while learning about Intelligent Design.

2. Agree to commit to an abstinence pledge at a Love Waits seminar. Leave curious about whether you can still masturbate and retain born-again status.

3. Take a zealous youth pastor's advice and throw out all secular CDs, except U2, and Kanye West, since the jury is still out on whether the latter is saved.

4. Get peer-pressured into speaking in tongues by a Pentecostal buddy while trapped in the boondocks at a church retreat. After learning how to babble in tongues, pressure another friend to join in by putting him or her in a headlock.

5. Begin carrying a Bible everywhere and start handing out religious tracts in the parking lot of the multiplex down by Sam Goody.

6. Discover you've developed that shiny, wholesome Jesus sparkle, just like the members of Jars of Clay. Begin saying "awesome" more frequently.

The idea of safe sex is a myth. It's like playing Russian roulette using one bullet instead of three. I don't have enough faith in a latex condom to believe it will protect me from HIV, man. Do you?

7. Get overcome by the spirit of Molsen Ice at Beach Week and almost break abstinence pledge, but stop yourself, thankfully, before going any further than oral sex.

8. Begin listening to crossover bands like Pedro the Lion and Sufjan Stevens after telling yourself there's no way God could like that contemporary Christian crap. Justify listening to 50 Cent's "In Da Club" by convincing yourself that "da Club" Fitty speaks of could be an awesome place to witness to non-Christians.

9. Begin seriously questioning your faith when you fall in love with a hell-bent liberal who turns you onto Buddhism and informs you that Bono has embraced teachings of "pagan" religions.

10. Abandon faith and/or repeat steps.

Evangelical *Vogue*: The Thomas Nelson BibleZines

When it comes to the bizarre, Thomas Nelson BibleZines take the cake. Claiming that "God isn't in a leather book," they set out to make the Bible more accessible to young people by repackaging the New Testament as a glossy fashion magazine. After all, teens and tweens are much more interested in clothes and dating than pharaohs and scrolls.

Revolve is Thomas Nelson Bible's first BibleZine. It was their response to typical Bible packaging, which is "too big and freaky looking." In addition to colorful sidebars condemning everything from abortion to homosexuality to Wiccanism, *Revolve* contains the complete New Testament coupled with fluffy dating advice and valuable beauty tips.

Revolve also contains recurring advice columns that answer questions like "When you repent, do you have to cry and stuff" and "My 'rents seem to think my belly button can lead to temptation . . . is that

Quick fact: Many evangelical and conservative groups have voiced opposition to a new vaccine that prevents the spread of genital warts, a virus that is a leading cause of cervical cancer. They feel that vaccinating preteens against the virus removes a useful deterrent to premarital sex.

(The New Yorker, 2006)

Revolve BibleZine

true?" An activities sidebar even has some romantic first-date suggestions, like "Take cookies to a nursing home."

Predictably, the horoscopes found in most secular fashion mags were omitted, since *Revolve* reminds us that "Astrology is totally condemned in the Scripture." The obligatory fashion magazine quiz, "Beneath the Sheets: Have You Ever Faked It?" was omitted as well.

Revolve became the bestselling Bible in America three months after its debut. The follow-up, *Revolve 2*, was released soon after. The publishers boast that the *Revolve* BibleZines appeal to the needs of contemporary teens. And with cutting-edge teachings like "God made guys to be the leaders" and "avoid heavy make-out sessions 'til you are married," who can argue with them?

QUICK QUIZ: Select the *Revolve* Girl Attribute *not* Listed in the BibleZine:

A. "Revolve girls don't call guys."
B. "Revolve girls have good posture."
C. "Revolve girls should never gossip."
D. "Revolve girls don't talk with food in their mouth."
E. "Revolve girls only put out for Christian suitors."

[Correct answer: E]

Evidently most commentary in *Revolve 2* was written by a seventy-five-year-old man from Kansas who wears a grease-stained wife beater, given troubling passages like this one: "God knows girls like to talk, and he needs to remind us to use our ears more than our mouths. Try to go a whole day without speaking."

Refuel is similar to *Revolve*, only for teen boys. Though unlike your typical magazine popular with pubescent boys, there are no naked women. In fact, masturbation is something God seems to frown upon given this passage found inside: "The Bible doesn't specifically address masturbation. But can it be separated from lust? The Bible forbids that, doesn't it? And besides, getting that kind of solo physical release

 Quick fact: The new "Christian" video game *Left Behind: Eternal Forces* encourages players to "wage a war of apocalyptic proportions" by blowing away Jews, Muslims, secular humanists, and other non-Christians who refuse to convert. The setting for the "spiritual warfare" is the sinful streets of New York, where the Antichrist's forces, known as the Global Community Peacekeepers, have taken power. Characters victoriously exclaim, "Praise the Lord" after violently slaughtering non-Christians.

(*Los Angeles Times and Talk2Action.org*, 2006)

What's that? BibleZines? You mean your so-called Messiah's book tailored for the teenage fools who peruse fashion magazines? Why, that's blasphemous, plain and simple. If you must pursue this "word," stick with good old-fashioned Aramaic script written on paper made from human skin.

is unhelpful because it trains you to be selfish about your sexuality." *Refuel* is also jam-packed with countless homophobic sidebars, like "Non-Girly Ways to Comfort a Friend," since evangelical teens need to learn how to be real men, like Dubya.

Real is a Thomas Nelson BibleZine for the hip-hop generation. It's King James Meets Queen Latifah. Inside, the authors warn against the evils of the Wu Tang Clan and Bone Thugs-N-Harmony, who they call "hellish," while reassuring readers that Jesus knew how to "keep it real":

"Did he [Jesus] only come for the rich folks in the suburbs or does he identify with folks on the street? Well, just look at his ancestors. He had a prostitute, a two-timing thug, and a player in his family tree. His mom and dad were exiles in Africa. . . . He kept his head up when the haters and pretenders took their best shots."

Highlights include the second chapter of Luke rewritten as a hip-hop rhyme, ongoing advice sidebars called "peep this," and an essay on how to overcome the thug life. On the downside, the 'zine appears to have been written by someone who learned about African-American culture by watching a Jay-Z video, given the inordinate amount of ink devoted to staying out of jail, coping with herpes, ditching your Glock, and, of course, keepin' it real.

Look for newer Thomas Nelson titles, including a Bible for fitness and health junkies and a bridal BibleZine.

HOLY SH!T!

Celebrity Evangelicals

Stephen Baldwin Host of an evangelical skateboarding ministry.

Willie Aames Former *Charles in Charge* star now plays Bibleman.

Mr. T I pity the fool who doesn't convert.

Bono U2 singer and missionary of peace.

Mase Former rapper is now Reverend Mason Betha.

M. C. Hammer Hosts his own Christian talk show.

Gary Busey He's not crazy, he's Christian.

George Foreman Former boxer now an ordained minister.

Kirk Cameron *Growing Pains* actor is now a televangelist and the star of the *Left Behind* movies.

Gloria Gaynor "I Will Survive" singer seeks eternal survival.

Al Green "Let's Stay Together" singer is now a pastor.

Cheryl Ladd Former *Charlie's Angel* has been on *The 700 Club*.

John Schneider Bo Duke is the founder of Faith Works Productions.

Smokey Robinson "I Second That Emotion" singer singing a new song.

Harry Reems *Deep Throat* star consummates a relationship with God.

Louis Gossett Jr. After starring in *Left Behind*, his Christian credentials were confirmed by his director.

John Tesh Former *Entertainment Tonight* host now records praise "music."

Lisa Whelchel *Facts of Life* bombshell got saved and wrote *So, You're Thinking About Homeschooling*.

Emerging Backlash,
the Other Emerging Church

Mark Driscoll, you scare us

It's unclear what the future holds for the evangelical right in America. Will evangelicals replace the Washington monument with a nine-hundred-foot Jesus statue? Will FOX News merge with *The 700 Club* and change their catchphrase from "No Spin Zone" to the more righteous "No Sin Zone"? Will most of the inhabitants of the red states vanish into thin air with the impending Rapture? Will Bibleman be revealed as the Antichrist and employ John Ashcroft as his right hand man?

One thing is for certain. Robertson, Dobson, LaHaye, Falwell, and the crusty evangelicals on Capitol Hill are all getting old. The evangelical right's future rests in the hands of its youth. Every time Dobson claims that the spoiled milk he found in his refrigerator is a sign of God's judgment on the homosexual agenda, young evangelicals become more and more alienated from the evangelical right's insanity. At least we would hope.

Even so, a vast number of evangelicals still remain, and let's be honest here, some of them are pretty scary. It's no wonder so many Americans have evangophobia. We only hope this guide has helped diminish some of that fear. As we said, we're here to help.

Fortunately, the Bush-questioning evangelicals at Calvin College, the progressive followers of Jim Wallis, and the Emerging Church Movement give us an inkling of hope. We'll have our sinning eyes on these up-and-coming evangelical progressives. That is, when we're not trying to destroy the foundation of heterosexual marriage or promoting the antifamily, freedom-hating agenda of the Beast.

The next generation of evangelical leaders, like Rob Bell and Brian McLaren, will decide the future . . .

. . . that is, unless the *other* side of the emerging church leads the march toward the impending Apocalypse.

Ladies and secular humanists, we'd like to introduce you to the

---

 Quick fact: The founder of Domino's Pizza, Tom Monaghan, is overseeing the construction of a five-thousand-acre planned community in Florida called Ave Maria. A devout Christian, Monaghan says Ave Maria will be a "Catholic Only" town, where pornography, abortion, condoms, and the pill will all be banned. Jeb Bush attended the groundbreaking. *(New York Times, 2006)*

emerging church's dark side, Mark Driscoll. Driscoll is the Seattle-based pastor who is Rob Bell's evil doppelganger, intent on spreading a gospel of doom to his youthful flock of evangelicals. Like Rob Bell, Driscoll is the pastor of an emerging church called Mars Hill. And notably, Rob Bell and Mark Driscoll were the two youngest pastors to be included on the Church Report's recent "50 most influential churches" list. Nevertheless, Bell is a progressive and Driscoll is, um, not. God help us if Driscoll helps define the future of evangelicalism.

Mark Driscoll: God Hates You

"God hates you," Pastor Mark Driscoll tells his congregation, the largest one in the state of Washington. Addressing a decidedly hip Gen X crowd of Christian scenesters, Driscoll warned his congregation that not everyone was going to like his sermon:

"God can't even look at us because he is so disgusted. . . . You have been told that God is loving, gracious, merciful, kind, compassionate, wonderful, and good. . . . That is a lie. . . . God looks down and says, 'I hate you, you are my enemy, and I will crush you.'"

A few minutes into the sermon—which spoke of God's "hatred" and "anger" over a hundred times—Driscoll confessed to his adoring young crowd that some people might be too offended to come back after hearing his fire-and-brimstone message.

Unfortunately, losing a few members is not a big concern for the thirty-something pastor. His Seattle-based Mars Hill Church has grown at a rate of 70 percent per year since opening in 1996. According to Driscoll, they added an additional eight hundred members—mainly trendy twenty-somethings "tapped into Seattle's underground scene"—in the previous month. He's more concerned about where to seat the impending overflow than about offending his audience.

Seattle is generally better known for its heathens and Wiccans than for its evangelicals. But Mars Hill Church has an appealing hook, bringing in large crowds in this decidedly blue state town. They operate a secular (albeit booze-free) "hardcore, punk, and indie" nightclub on the same grounds as the church, known as Paradox. They've hosted over seven hundred shows with headlining bands that include college radio favorites

Modest Mouse, Death Cab for Cutie, Bright Eyes, and Low. "This is an indie town," say Driscoll. "And Mars Hill is an indie church."

There's never any preaching or proselytizing at Paradox. Driscoll doesn't want to pull a "bait and switch," he says. Unfortunately, the bait and switch of Mars Hill Church is Driscoll himself. He goes out of his way to seem hip and appealing, but the intolerant doomsday gospel he preaches conjures up visions of a tragic Great White show. Keep your children away from him before he brings out the strychnine cocktails or takes to the stage at Paradox singing his own doctored version of "Jesus Loves You"—like he did recently during a sermon at Mars Hill. "Jesus hates me, it is so," Driscoll sang, mocking what he believes to be the song's inherent naïveté. He's a Paradox indeed. And by "paradox" we mean "douchebag."

Most Inane Mark Driscoll Quote: "After church tonight you will go home and you will eat chicken, not human, because of the spread of Christianity . . . go to a country where there hasn't been the spread of Christianity and they're having human for dinner."

A New Kind of Falwell: The Emerging Fundamentalist

Driscoll says he hates the "F" word, which surprised us given his fondness for its derivatives, "friggin'" and "freakin'." "I'm a freakin' Bible thumper," he claims. Still, the "F" word Driscoll is referring to is "fundamentalist." The word reminds him of "backwoods preachers" obsessed with alcohol and sexual mores. Driscoll's got no problem with alcohol in moderation, and when it comes to sex he's lectured married couples on blow jobs and "how to have a good orgasm." It's a topic that we're delighted, frankly, that fundamentalists like Jerry Falwell have never broached.

But Driscoll's appeal to the young people of Seattle seems to reside in his unorthodox breed of fundamentalism. "I'm theologically conservative and culturally liberal," he says. "Frankly I think it confuses a lot of people." His description of himself all sounds perfectly appealing. That is, until you hear Driscoll claim that Jesus was no "limp-wristed hippie" who came to earth "wearing a robe like some fairy," as he did in a recent sermon. Not surprisingly, Driscoll has been described as a frat boy too.

Driscoll Says He's Not a Fundamentalist.
You Decide . . .

- Says he's seen possessed people "totally overtaken" by demons "levitate off the ground."
- Believes the Bible literally and says homosexuality is a sin.
- Doesn't believe in evolution and invited the Discovery Institute to lecture at his church.
- Refuses to let women become church elders and says they should get spousal approval from their dads before marrying.
- Claims "Jesus is a God who hates."
- Believes most people are *predestined* by God to spend eternity "smoldering" in hell, a place of "torment with burning sulfur."
- Presumably enjoys stepping on flowers and throwing rocks at bunny rabbits.

Onward Christian Soldiers

Unlike leaders of the evangelical right, Driscoll thankfully says he wants to stay out of politics. He's more interested in condemning people to hell *on a grassroots level.* Among the group of young pastors credited for creating the Emerging Church Movement, Driscoll's Club Paradox embodies the movement's attempts to find new ways to evangelize Gen Xers. Still, Driscoll has since become the movement's Judas, warning progressive evangelicals to avoid "drinking from the emerging church toilet."

Driscoll even criticizes the emerging movement's leader, Brian McLaren, for being a peacemaker: "Conflict, war, and violence deeply troubles [McLaren]," says Driscoll. "A pacifist has a lot of difficulty reconciling pacifism with scripture." Driscoll calls leaders of the emerging movement, such as Rob Bell and Brian McLaren, "disgrun-

 Quick fact: "You, therefore, have no excuse, you who pass judgment on someone else, for at whatever point you judge the other, you are condemning yourself, because you who pass judgment do the same things."   (Romans 2:1, The Bible)

tled liberal evangelicals who gather together to complain about the megachurches of their parents." They're what Driscoll calls his "big beef."

"If you look at the [other] guys in the emerging church," he says, "they have a lot of ideas, but they don't have a lot of converts . . . I'm converting the lost and seeing life transformations by the thousands."

Praise Jesus, Mark! Getting converts is what being an evangelical is about. After all, that's why we call you an evangelical, instead of a Christian.

The Evangelical Quiz:
Test Your Knowledge

1. According to most evangelicals, which one of the following is not a sign of the last days?

   A. Floods, earthquakes, and other natural disasters
   B. The spread of false prophets
   C. "Jesus is my Homeboy" T-shirt line finds success at Urban Outfitters
   D. The 1948 creation of the state of Israel

2. Which of the following posters can be found in former Republican Congressman Tom Delay's work office?

   A. White Snake performing a show at the Hampton Coliseum in '86
   B. The Coors Light twins
   C. A Rapture poster with the words: "This Could Be the Day"
   D. An original *Teen Wolf 2* movie poster signed by Justin Bateman

3. *Plugged In,* Focus on the Family's movie magazine, criticized *all but one* of the following movies for promoting something they refer to as "outercourse." Choose the supposedly outercourse-free film.

   A. *Kinsey*
   B. *40 Days and 40 Nights*
   C. *The 40-Year-Old Virgin*
   D. *Anchorman: The Legend of Ron Burgundy*

4. Choose the item that James Dobson *was not* beaten and/or disciplined with, according to his book *Dare to Discipline*.

    A. straps and buckles
    B. a girdle
    C. a shoe
    D. tongs
    E. twigs and branches

5. True or False, Ted Haggard, head of the National Association of Evangelicals, has a "Vote for Pedro" bumper sticker on his truck, from the film *Napoleon Dynamite*.

    A. True
    B. False

6. Which of the following *is* a book in the Old Testament?

    A. The Gospel of Yolanda
    B. Malakadiah
    C. The Early Years: Arks, Floods, Tablets, and a Naked Chick in Paradise
    D. Reagan
    E. Haggai

7. What Would Jesus Do (WWJD): A sick gay man can't afford health insurance without getting on a shared plan with his partner:

    A. Say, "You don't get no special rights, faggot"
    B. Heal him and then try to help him afford insurance

8. WWJD: When approaching a homeless man who is hungry:

    A. Yell "get a job, hippie," complain about welfare, and then go watch the Packers game with John the Baptist
    B. Give him food

9. How many senators received a perfect voting score from the Christian Coalition according to a report released by the group prior to the 2006 midterm elections?

   A. 42
   B. All of them
   C. 15
   D. 33
   E. 250

10. What term do evangelicals use as a synonym for environmentalism?

   A. The Hippie Agenda
   B. Satanism
   C. Creation Care
   D. Garden Grooming
   E. Capitalism

11. According to Ted Haggard, how can we solve the world's environmental problems?

   A. Stop relying on the brainpower of "socialist" environmentalists
   B. Promote a pro-business economy
   C. Get the leaders of Wal-Mart and Coke together in a room to determine a solution
   D. All of the above

12. Which pair of contiguous states have the lowest number of churchgoers?

   A. New York and Vermont
   B. Oregon and Washington
   C. North Carolina and South Carolina
   D. Vermont and Massachusetts
   E. Maine and New Hampshire

13. Jerry Jenkins, coauthor of the *Left Behind* series, authored which of the following comics from 1996 to 2004?

A. *AntiChristman*
B. *Gil Thorpe*
C. *The Family Circus*
D. *Batman Born Again*
E. *The X-Sinning X-Men*

14. True or False: The divorce rate is higher in red states than blue states?

A. True
B. False

15. Which one of the following *is not* a gay deprogramming and/or "ex-gay" group?

A. Love Won Out
B. Exodus International
C. Homosexuals Anonymous
D. FAG—The Foundation Against Gays
E. Love in Action

16. True or False: George W. Bush declared June 10 to be "Jesus Day" when he was governor of Texas?

A. True
B. False

17. Chick-fil-A's cited "first priority" is which of the following:

A. "To get around to changing that grease that's been backed up in the fryer since 1988."
B. "To do Chik-fil-A's Chick-n-Strips Right."
C. "To Fil-A-Artery with divinely anointed fried chicken grease."

D. "To serve a higher calling."

E. "To baptize you in oil."

18. According to Gallup, what percentage of Americans say they would not be upset if Creationism were taught in public school?

    A. 34%

    B. 54%

    C. 76%

    D. 81%

19. Which popular children's character did Jerry Falwell accuse of being gay?

    A. SpongeBob SquarePants

    B. Aquaman

    C. Barney

    D. Pee-wee Herman

    E. Tinky Winky

20. Which foreign country's leader did Pat Robertson say we should assassinate?

    A. Venezuela

    B. Colombia

    C. Bolivia

    D. France

[Correct answers: 1. C, 2. C, 3. D, 4. D, 5. A, 6. E, 7. B, 8. B, 9. A, 10. C, 11. D, 12. B, 13. B, 14. A, 15. D, 16. A, 17. D, 18. C, 19. E, 20. A]

Christianese:
An Evangelical Glossary

Affliction: Preferred term for any form of sickness, since it implies an outside force (Satan) trying to impose his will. Saying you're "sick" sounds mundane. Claiming you have an affliction, now that's some Old Testament shit.

Anointed: Oil is an important sacrament to many Christians and explains their love of suburban franchises like Red Lobster and, presumably, their support of candidates with ties to Saudi Arabian oil moguls. Anointing with oil is a common evangelical ritual designating that something is set apart for the Lord's use. Evangelicals often literally anoint themselves, church buildings, and even government buildings to assure God's blessing.

To be anointed: Having God's blessing
Sentence: "I saved a dollar on Honey Bunches of Oats cereal at Wal-Mart. My good fortune must be the anointing of God!"

Antichrist: A Satanic being who, according to many evangelicals, will soon reveal himself and become ruler of a one-world Socialist government. Also, Bill Clinton.

Armageddon: The climax of the Antichrist's temporary rule of the earth. The final battle in which Jesus defeats Satan. Also, the worst Michael Bay movie ever made. Incidentally, many believe the successful career of Michael *"Bad Boys II"* Bay is a sign of the last days.

Backsliding: To return to a sin you'd once overcome, like smoking, sexual promiscuity, drugs, or watching violent R-rated movies that *were not* made by Mel Gibson.

Sentence: "We saw his car in the Target parking lot despite their war on Christmas. He's backsliding."

Baptized in the Spirit/Spirit-filled: When evangelicals become born again, they believe the Holy Spirit *literally* lives inside them, right next to the turkey Reuben they're digesting. *Spirit-filled* evangelicals got served an extra scoop of Holy Spirit at God's Heavenly buffet. And with more Holy Spirit living inside them, they also receive Divine "gifts" or "fruits" of the Spirit, like speaking in tongues, healing, Divine words of knowledge, prophecy, and, sometimes, licorice.

Bathsheba/Jezebel: Women who wear halter tops to the Sunday service. Bathsheba and Jezebel were the *Girls Gone Wild* of Moses's time.

Being a witness: Showing sinners the desirability of the Christian life with loving actions.

Sentence: "My nonjudgmental friendship is a good witness to Megan. Hopefully it will inspire her to stop sinning so she won't have to spend eternity burning in a pool of flame."

Bible-believin' church: A literal-minded church that believes the entire Bible, even the creepy parts. *Antonym:* Facts-believin' church

Sentence: "We ain't no Methodists! We're Bible-believin'!"

Blessed: The essential code term for Christians. Popular usages: *Have a blessed day* and *God bless you.* Turning blessed into a two-syllable word, like in *bless-ed be the Lord,* suggests you're really down with J.C. *I'm blessed* is the correct response to give to another evangelical who asks "How are you?"; otherwise they may lay hands on you and begin praying.

Born-again/Saved: Someone who has accepted Jesus into his or her heart and will spend eternity in Heaven, a magical place where there are no Catholics, taxes, or nonfranchise restaurants.

Covered by the blood: Protected by the blood of the cross, having Jesus's protection.

Sentence: Jim: "Hey, Mike, shouldn't you wear a seat belt if you're gonna drive this fast?"
Mike: "Don't worry, Jim, I'm covered by the blood."

Creation Care: The evangelical word for environmentalism. Similarly, *shut-up, hippie* is their term for *global warming*.

Sentence: "Do milk cartons go in the blue creation care bags, or with the regular trash?"

The Elected: A Calvinist belief common among Presbyterians and some Baptists that there is no free will. Instead, God has predestined some to be saved, and others—mainly people who listen to rock music and drive hybrids—to spend an eternity in flame. You know, favoritism.

The Emerging Church: A movement among young evangelicals— who are fed up with crappy Christian Rock, the evangelical right, and churches with waterslides—to make Christianity relevant and post-modern.

Evangelical: Christians who claim to have a personal relationship

 Quick fact: The federal government spends an estimated $170 million per year to spread their abstinence-only message. By federal law, abstinence programs cannot promote condoms. They can only discuss condoms' failure rates and their ineffectiveness in the prevention of disease and pregnancy. *(60 Minutes, 2005)*

with Jesus Christ, think the Bible is infallible, and feel God wants them to spread His word to others. Most evangelicals are cultural conservatives who believe the Holy Spirit literally lives inside them. They tend to enjoy the type of music one hears on *Star Search* reruns.

Evangophobia: The fear of evangelicals.

Fellowship: Christians don't hang out. They "have fellowship." And usually while sharing Reese's Pieces Sundaes at Friendly's.

The Flesh: Something of a sinful or unspiritual nature, especially of a sexual nature. Also, a short-lived Christian goth band rebelliously named by the pastor's sullen daughter, who wears black fishnet stockings to the Saturday night youth service.

Flock: A church's congregation. The preferred term for a group of Christians to gaggle, herd, coven, and RNC.

Fruit: The tangible rewards associated with devotion to God.

Sentence: "The Packers' overtime victory yesterday was the fruit of my prayer."

Full gospel church: Simply means, our services are like ecstatic raves, only we're all high on the Holy Spirit, we like to babble in tongues, and we think techno is the devil's music.

Fundamentalist: Evangelicals who believe the Bible is literally true, avoid stuff like alcohol and R-rated movies, and say "you're wrong, because the Bible says so" a lot.

Get your praise on: The evangelical equivalent of "are you ready to rock?!" Popular with youth ministers who have goatees and an earring.

Sentence: "Are you ready to get your praise on, people! DJ Sin X-Peller will be out here in a minute spinning some righteously rockin' praise 'n' worship hits. Can you say Jesus is Alive! Amen Amen."

God is a God of deliverance: A popular catchphrase. It means God can lead you through troubled situations. As opposed to the less popular phrase *God is a Beach*.

Great Commission: The belief that God's most important teaching is Matthew 28:18–20, where he tells his disciples to evangelize the whole world. Second only to the Greater Commission, which tells them to boycott companies affiliated with the making of *The Da Vinci Code*.

Hallelujah, Glory, Amen, and Praise the Lord: Interchangeable words to be shouted aloud in church when feeling all tingly with Jesus. Less popular substitutions: hip hip hooray, bravo, yay, Fuck yeah!

How's your walk?: Christian shorthand for "How's your walk with God?" It's like asking "How's it hanging?" you know, without all that scrotum.

Intelligent Design: The belief that Darwinism is improbable since it would take an intelligent God to create something as intricate as human beings. After all, complex sentient beings who lounge on the sofa in their underwear eating bags of Cheetos while they watch *Everybody Loves Raymond* couldn't have possibly evolved from dumb monkeys. Also known as *Creationism*.

Let go and let God: A popular evangelical phrase that means *Don't worry about it, God will take care of it*. Also, a popular evangelical welfare policy.

Sentence: Jim: "This is embarrassing, Mike, but I think my wife slept with

---

 Quick fact: Yoido Full Gospel Church in Seoul, South Korea, has over 780,000 members, roughly half the population of Philadelphia. It's the largest evangelical congregation in the world. *(Arkansas Democrat-Gazette, 2006)*

---

someone else because of my erectile dysfunction disorder."
Mike: "It'll be okay, Jim, let go and let God."

Liberal: Sinner. Someone who wants to raise your taxes and prevent you from being able to afford that big-screen TV from Sharper Image. Similar to the way Eskimos have multiple words for the word "snow," evangelicals have many for the word "liberal."

Here are a few: *New York Times* reader, Card-carrying ACLU member, Intellectual, latte drinker, Yankee, city slicker, MoveOn.org supporter, sushi eater, moral relativist, windsurfer, secular elitist, secular humanist, Hillary supporter, French, faggot.

Mainline denominations: The fastly diminishing group of denominations: United Methodist Church, Episcopal Church, Evangelical Lutheran Church in America, Presbyterian Church USA, United Church of Christ. Many evangelicals say mainline denominations are on the decline since they've become more liberal, though studies suggest it's those flavorless Communion wafers and Deacon Willy's biscuits-'n'-gravy breath.

Media elite: Any secular media outlet other than FOX News, *Reader's Digest*, the *Washington Times*, and *Guideposts*. (See *Liberal*.)

Megachurch: An evangelical church with two thousand or more regular attendees and/or a Frappuccino counter.

New Age: Pagan- and Eastern-inspired spirituality controlled by Satan, such as crystal healing, astrology, and the music they play in Dottie's Age of Aquarius Book Store.

Sentence: "Lydia drives a hybrid, drinks only filtered water, and buys her potpourri from Pier 1 imports. She must be a New Ager!"

Pentecostals/Charismatics: The fastest-growing branch of Christianity, which includes many denominations, such as the popular Assembly of God. They're the "spirit-filled" ones who speak in tongues, hear voices, TiVo Benny Hinn, and think the graffiti on the building down by the old creek is the work of a demonic coven. Pentecostal and Charismatic churches all have a born-again Deadhead who used to work at a headshop named Scarlet Begonias but got born again after Jerry Garcia died.

Political Correctness: Allowing gays, women, and other religions *special* rights like equal pay and health care.

Praise-and-worship: The part of an evangelical's church service where Lite FM "praise" songs are sung and hands are lifted upward toward Heaven. Lyrics are generally projected onto a movie screen. Sometimes state-of-the-art video projections of gleeful children with bowl cuts running through heavenly fields of wheat are included for added effect.

Prayer Warrior: Someone who's kick-ass at praying.

Sentence: "Back off, Lydia, you don't know what you're dealing with. I've slayed demons with prayer. I'm a prayer warrior. Don't frig with me, lady."

Prayerwalk: Going to a designated area to walk and pray for God's blessing. Common sites for prayerwalks include government buildings, bar/crime districts, sites intended for churches, and places that have been designated demonic because a local goth killed a squirrel there. Prayerdriving and prayerrunning take less time, but aren't as effective.

Sentence: Mike: "Hey, Jim, do you want to go for a prayerwalk in the neighborhood after work?"
Jim: "That's okay, Mike, I'm going to do some prayer cardio on the treadmill."

Premillennialism: The most popular end-times scenario, as envisioned in the *Left Behind* books and their film adaptations starring Kirk Cameron from *Growing Pains*. Premillennialists think end-times events will unfold in this order: (1) The Rapture; (2) the rise of the Antichrist; (3) Jesus will return to set up a kingdom on Earth for a Millennium. Then, Alan Thicke, Joanna Kerns, Kirk Cameron, Tracey Gold, and the rest of the *Growing Pains* gang will forgive the Antichrist and let him have a cameo as a wacky neighbor in a reunion special.

Pro-Family: An advocate of the traditional, nuclear, one-income, meatloaf-eating, Dave Barry–reading family. *Antonym:* family hater

Prosperity Gospel: The belief that the all-powerful God allowed Himself to be nailed to a cross by a heckling crowd of sandal wearers so that their born-again offspring—at least the self-righteous, extra-devoted ones who give money to televangelists—could all own brand-new Ford Explorers and McMansions. *Similar:* **Seed faith** Giving money to a ministry (planting a seed) with the expectation of a larger harvest (an all-expense-paid trip on a Carnival Cruise of the Caribbean).

Rapture: Before Armageddon and the reign of the Antichrist, evangelicals believe they will ascend into heaven, without warning, to be spared the trauma of the last days. Incidentally, evangelicals know your hair can get all blown to hell when you're catapulted into Heaven. This is why they wear so much hairspray.

Sentence: Harold: "Should we use Fandango to buy our movie tickets in advance?"
Sally: "Are you crazy, Harold?! What if we get Raptured on the way to the theater?"

Reparative therapy: The term evangelicals use for the brainwashing classes they send gays and lesbians to when they want to get the gay out. Want to become a so-called ex-gay? Did you sympathize with the characters in *Brokeback Mountain*? Are you one of the many men who slept with SpongeBob SquarePants? You may need some reparative therapy.

Reconstructionism: The belief that the Founding Fathers wanted America to be a Christian nation with nativity scenes and "Footprints in the Sand" plaques in its legislative buildings and courthouses.

Seeker-Sensitive: A church or church service designed to appeal to the "unchurched," though none of the ones we've visited offer a cocktail hour or hard liquor.

Slain in the spirit: To be profoundly moved (or even physically lose consciousness) due to an encounter with the Holy Spirit. Common when touched by a healer or in need of a nap at church.

Sentence: "He was going to take my space in the parking lot but decided not to at the last minute. God must have slain him in the spirit."

Small groups (a.k.a. cell groups): Most large churches encourage people to join a small group, which often meet in people's homes, to strengthen bonds to the church and to make them feel like they belong to a community. New Life Church in Colorado Springs has an estimated fifteen thousand church-affiliated small groups, including Praise Aerobics, Worship Hula, Biblical Creationism vs. Evolution, Volleyball with James (where you play volleyball as a warm-up to studying James), and our favorite, an arts group called Mom & Me Rubber-Stamping.

Sodomite: A homosexual. *Synonyms:* abomination, Elton John.

Speak in Tongues: A very common "spiritual gift" that allows evangelicals to speak aloud using the language of the Lord. Sometimes known as gibberish. Often, evangelicals with a Divine gift of "interpretation" can provide a translation of tongues. Similarly, *praying in tongues* is a more personal, quieter form of tongues commonly used by evangelicals for personal edification. It's recommended that you don't gossip or mumble in tongues, since no one likes gossips and mumblers. If you want to fake it, just say "meca-leka, hi meca hiny-ho."

Spiritual warfare: When one is in battle with the supernatural forces of evil. Spiritual Warfare would also be a fantastic name for a Christian paintball company.

Sentence: "I'm in spiritual warfare with that Yankee pharmacist at Duane Reade. He always takes forever to fill my Celebrex prescription because he didn't like it when I told him I was praying he'd take that Vote Democrat sticker off his truck."

Standing on the promises: A common idiomatic expression that means you have faith in God's promise that He blesses his followers.

Sentence: "I'm not sure 7-Eleven will accept this Fruit Roll-Ups coupon, but I'm standing on the promises."

Testimony: One's anecdotal history about getting saved or one's spiritual journey.

Sentence: "I hate my lame testimony. I got saved watching 700 Club *one night when I was depressed about Rhonda leaving me for that dude with the Lexus. Big freakin' whoop!"*

Tithe: To give 10 percent of your wealth to the church. A prerequisite to being a good Christian and something that is commonly required of evangelicals who want to become members of a church.

Sentence: "If we base our tithes on our pretaxed gross earnings, Harold, will we get a refund from God at the end of the year in addition to all our other blessings?"

Tongues: See *Speak in tongues.*

Word of Knowledge: Belief that Jesus is communicating something directly to you that is meant to be shared with others. One of the gifts of the holy spirit. *Common phrase:* "I have a Word for you."

Sentence:
Pat Robertson's sidekick with stiff hair: "What's going on in the news, Pat?"
Pat Robertson paraphrase: "I have a Word of Knowledge that God wants Hugo Chavez assassinated."

Our Statement of Beliefs

All evangelical ministries post a Statement of Beliefs. Here's ours:

WE BELIEVE . . . Jesus was a progressive liberal.

WE BELIEVE . . . Love the political ministry, hate the tax exemption.

WE BELIEVE . . . Jesus hates Christian Rock, Pat Robertson diet shakes, and pastors who pronounce his name "Jay-sus."

WE BELIEVE . . . Wearing WWJD (What Would Jesus Do?) and NOTW (Not of This World) logos is AGWTEA (A Great Way to Ensure Abstinence).

WE BELIEVE . . . Good deeds with a conversion agenda are not good deeds.

WE BELIEVE . . . The church's biggest heresy can be summed up in six words: *John Tesh: Worship at Red Rocks*.

WE BELIEVE . . . Malachi is an inspirational book in the Old Testament, but he also ruled in the movie *Children of the Corn*.

WE BELIEVE . . . Christianity is no better than Buddhism, Hinduism, Islam, or Judaism. It does kick Scientology's ass, though.

WE BELIEVE . . . *Eternal* condemnation for *finite* sin?! And you actually want us to endorse your Supreme Court picks?

WE BELIEVE . . . We're not antifamily. We're anti-Bush family.

WE BELIEVE . . . The good ole days when sensible folk could make fun of the French without feeling like right-wing nut jobs will probably never return.

WE BELIEVE . . . *The Passion of the Christ* is a horrible, horrible movie.

WE BELIEVE . . . Your choir director is probably gay too, so get over it.

WE BELIEVE . . . Sin is in the eye of the beholder.

Acknowledgments

Special thanks to my rapturous angel, Amy Brown, for inspiration, editing, and personal salvation. To Kevin Kraynick, minister of Catch.com, for the cover concept. To the demon-possessed Matthew Casper, who transcribed the words of Ronnie James Dio. To Bret Nicely for his heavenly assistance with the evangelical hairdos and assorted swine. To Jud Laghi for making the magic happen, even though magic is satanic. To my editor, Mark Chait, for his anointed help. To Jeff Campbell (A.K.A. Teen Wolf), the deacon of aesthetics. And as always, a special thanks to Jeff Bechtel, the most sinfully talented man I know. This book could not have been written without the support, tips, and creative suggestions of my prayer warriors: John Rickman, Cameron O'Brion, Glenn Stevens, Judy Coan-Stevens, Kristen Fulton-Wright, Shaun Wright, Blabio, Pete Thompson, Ben Stokes, Adrianne Lanham, Apryl Prentiss, Andy and Laura Garnett-Wall, Steve Brown, Judy Brown, Anna Brown, Colin Cheney, Mischa, Austin Welder, Noah Sussman, Chris Nespor, Joanna Burgess, Chris O'Brion, Joe Decker, Ryland Sanders, Monte Holman, William Newhouse, and Arturo Herrera. I miss you, Jane. If there's a Heaven, you're there.

Michael Moore: Winner of the Coveted
"Most Likely To Burn in Hell" Award

About the Author

Robert Lanham was raised in Richmond, Virginia, in the heart of the Bible Belt, where he attended a strict Southern Baptist church. He grew up in an environment where rock music was considered the devil's music and with parents who speak in tongues, vote Republican, and have a vanity plate that says *Prayzin*. Lanham's first babysitter was Republican senator Tom Coburn, best known for advocating the death penalty for abortion providers. As a teen, before his fall from grace, Lanham tried to speak in tongues, but failed. Lanham now lives in the den of iniquity, New York City. Despite the prayers and efforts of many, Lanham did not get "saved" during the course of this study, but is confident he'll be just fine. He's the author of *The Hipster Handbook* and *Food Court Druids, Cherohonkees and other Creatures Unique to the Republic* and is the editor and founder of FREEwilliamsburg.com.

About the Artist

Jeff Bechtel grew up in Richmond as well—the one in Indiana. Raised in a household where there was little mention of God, religion was bewildering to Bechtel. He recalls being scorned by a religious fanatic for buying the *Dungeons & Dragons Player's Handbook* as a child and hearing disturbing tales about cult leader Jim Jones, another native of Richmond, Indiana. Making sure he avoided Kool-Aid, Bechtel ran off to art school before eventually moving to Brooklyn, New York, to become a draftsman for hire. Bechtel has drawn weird pictures for Robert Lanham's past two books. He remains among the lost, destined to be left behind should the Rapture arrive.

James Dobson—The Evangelical Pope

Jerry Falwell—TheTourettesVangelist

Ted Haggard—The Duke of Haggard

George Bush—Commander in Chief

Pat Robertson—The Godfather